PRAISE FOR

# *HEALING WITHOUT FORGIVING*



"A fresh and sympathetic contribution to trauma recovery literature." —***Kirkus Reviews***

"I have been both moved and enlightened by Lyn's book, *Healing Without Forgiving*. She has masterfully revealed the process of healing for dissociative survivors of childhood trauma. Her approach has transformed the way I do spiritual counseling and has taught me new insights into the process of healing, respecting the real needs of individuals while revealing some of the hurtful mistakes that come from preconceived patterns about religion and spirituality."

—**Peter Chepaitis**, OFM, Franciscan Catholic priest of the Province of Our Lady of Guadalupe, cofounder of Bethany Ministries (www.bethmin.org)

"I picked up Lyn Barrett's book, *Healing Without Forgiving: A Hero's Journey for Dissociative Survivors*, out of curiosity. I have been a clinical psychologist for fifty years and have treated many trauma survivors, but, using the DSM criteria, thought I had never encountered dissociation in my practice. After reading Ms. Barrett's engrossing volume, I am now not so sure. . . . Ms. Barrett has opened a door for me for further exploration of my trauma symptoms, which continue to this day, and I am eighty-three years old. I wholeheartedly recommend this book to any trauma survivor or relative or friend of one."

—**Ronald F. Levant**, EdD, LP, ABPP, professor of psychology emeritus at the University of Akron, former president of the American Psychological Association

"This is the book that survivors of chronic childhood trauma have been waiting for to free them from the ubiquitous cultural and religious expectation that forgiving our perpetrators is the goal of healing. Through a brilliant guide for survivors, therapists, and helpers, Lyn illustrates that forgiveness of our offender(s) is just one path within the larger container of healing. Packed with stories by dissociative survivors and self-reflective exercises, this is a book meant to be a companion along the healing journey."

—**Linda Crockett**, founder of Safe Communities and author of *The Deepest Wound: How a Journey to El Salvador Led to Healing from Mother-Daughter Incest*

"An excellent resource! *Healing Without Forgiving* addresses the complexities that surround forgiveness through survivor stories, identifying societal and internalized pressures, and encouraging personal reflection. This is a gift for all 'heroes' on their journey of healing from trauma."

—**Kay Johnson**, LICSW psychotherapist, specializing in healing from complex trauma

"Based on best therapeutic practices, sound research, and years of learning through personal experience, Ms. Barrett has created a valuable workbook that is adaptable to individual recovery from dissociative identity disorder. Her work exemplifies the basic principles and values of social work, especially that of helping people identify their own strengths to become, as she says, 'the heroes of their own stories.'"

—**Lorraine A. Libby**, MSW, adjunct professor (Ret.),
Central Connecticut State University

"*Healing Without Forgiving* is an invitation to live a whole life. Wholeness involves embracing the totality of your experience, the dark and the light, the healed and the unhealed. Contrary to common but often superficial wisdom, Lyn Barrett asserts that healing does not require forgiving the perpetrators of evil and trauma but coming to realize that you are beautiful and beloved in all your imperfections and struggles. Although this text is chock-full of exercises aimed at experiencing self-awareness and wholeness, *Healing Without Forgiving* is more than a how-to workbook. Lyn Barrett presents a path of life that invites each of us to embark on our own heroic healing journey. Recognizing that each of our journeys to wholeness is unique, Barrett provides a road to self-awareness not only for persons diagnosed with dissociative identity disorders but all of us who seek healing of the trauma that touches every life and who desire to be supportive of those who experience dissociative disorders. I highly recommend this book for persons with dissociative disorders, therapists, pastors, and those who seek to heal themselves and become supportive companions of dissociative survivors."

—**Bruce Epperly**, PhD, author of *Jesus: Mystic, Healer, and Prophet*

"Lyn Barrett wrote her first book to help us understand dissociative identity disorder. In this book she guides the reader toward a healing in which forgiving the perpetrator is not essential. The wisdom of this book is useful to both those who suffer from DID and others who struggle with forgiveness. Drawing upon her vast expert knowledge, she combines compassion with clear thinking in helping us understand how forgiveness is not an essential ingredient for healing. Her background in education, theology, and writing combines with expert information drawn from psychology, psychiatry, and neuroscience to provide a path forward for those who have been victimized and suffer from trauma. I have known Lyn Barrett for a decade—and worked with her on a research project—and continue to be impressed by her insight and ability to promote a healing environment."

—**Michael Crabtree**, PhD, licensed psychologist, researcher, and professor of psychology at Washington & Jefferson College

"Lyn Barrett's *Healing Without Forgiving* offers a new approach to overcoming trauma that doesn't include forgiving, or, more precisely, doesn't include forgiving if it 'isn't right for me.' That distinction is the real power of her book: giving permission for those seeking to heal to set their unique intention and forge the path that is right for them. I do not have dissociative identity disorder, but Barrett's prescription for individualized healing from DID mirrors my fight to take back my health: charting my own path by not listening to societal norms telling me I was 'just getting old,' realizing that forward movement is a journey (not always a linear one), recognizing that small successes keep us moving forward, finding ways to fit our work into everyday demands, acknowledging the power of gratitude, and always, always maintaining hope. Barrett shows how those dealing with DID can live into their 'deepest longings' and 'desired intention'—all to capture the power and joy of deciding 'who they will be.'"

—**Kathy Bauernfeind**, author of *Don't Give In! (You're Not Just Getting Old)*

"Author Lyn Barrett invites readers to step up, center stage, into the spotlight of forgiving, raising the dark, heavy curtains of dissociative trauma into the public eye. *Healing Without Forgiveness: A Hero's Journey for Dissociative Survivors* takes a front row seat for those weighed down by childhood pain, a topic that is often brushed aside, buried deep, or erased due to discomfort and anguish in addressing the past. This workbook speaks to the important message of healing regardless of the adversity. The collection of twenty-six exercises focuses on self-reflection, dealing with heavy burdens, acknowledgment of emotional or physical damage, thoughtful perspectives, confronting forgiveness, and, of course, opening old wounds. The Healing Wheel is a road map to recovery. As readers dig deep to unveil and address their feelings, their ticket to healing is in the hard effort it takes to work through emotional issues triggered in their childhood. A must-read for those seeking insights and coping strategies for inner strength to create a healthy future, closing the curtains on a stormy time."

—**Letitia E. Hart**, author of *Reach Out with Acts of Kindness: A Guide to Helping Others in Crisis*

"As both a healer and someone still navigating the layers of my own childhood trauma, I recognize how complex the journey of conceptualizing forgiveness can be. As survivors, we often find ourselves returning to this question again and again, wrestling with it in ways both conscious and subtle. In this book, Lyn doesn't claim to have all the answers; instead, she meets the reader exactly where they are by acknowledging the struggle, the pain, and the courage it takes to reflect on the offering of forgiveness, whether to ourselves or others. She invites us to approach forgiveness as a living, creative practice—something to engage with thoughtfully and gently, rather than as a requirement on the path to healing."

—**Brandi Gurcak**, MS, LPC

*Healing Without Forgiving:*
*A Hero's Journey for Dissociative Survivors*

by Lyn Barrett



ISBN 979-8-88824-939-0



Illustrated by Gwen Vogel

Cover and book design by Lauren Sheldon

Published by

köehlerbooks™

3705 Shore Drive
Virginia Beach, VA 23455
800-435-4811
www.koehlerbooks.com

# HEALING WITHOUT FORGIVING

A Hero's Journey for Dissociative Survivors

LYN BARRETT

Foreword by Dr. Jamie Marich

VIRGINIA BEACH
CAPE CHARLES

*Dedicated to Suritaplus*
*and to the community of Dissociative Writers,*
*who are true heroes.*

# TABLE OF CONTENTS

# ACKNOWLEDGMENTS

This workbook is a collaboration of many voices. I'd like to thank all those who filled out questionnaires, participated in focus groups, sat for interviews, and gave me permission to put their thoughts into print. Most of the voices on these pages are in their own name, but a few have chosen a part's or another agreeable name; all of these voices include Aces, Barbie, Bonnie, Cathy, Gabby, Jaime, Jamie, Janice, Jayden, Judie, Kim, Michael, Sarah, Sharon, Sharri, Shelley, Surita, and Tanya. While each voice is different, each is valuable and contributes to the overall fabric and feel of *Healing Without Forgiving: A Hero's Journey for Dissociative Survivors.*

I'm especially grateful to Suritaplus, Sharon, Jamie Marich (The Unicorn System), Sharri, Bonnie Armstrong, and Jamie Michelle Pollock for allowing me to highlight the ways in which they grappled with forgiving their perpetrators through their stories at the end of each chapter. These more in-depth narratives put flesh on the thesis of *Healing Without Forgiving* and show the variety of responses survivors have when confronted with the issue of forgiveness. A special thanks to Jamie Marich, again, for writing the foreword to this workbook. Jamie's vast experience as a person with dissociative identities, as well as a clinician who works with dissociative survivors, lends weight to her affirmation.

Several beta readers gave me important suggestions that prompted changes in the text or graphics, including Gabby, Lorraine Libby, Shelley Kolton, Michael Crabtree, and Father Peter Chepaitis. Although this workbook is intentionally not Christian in orientation, Friar Peter reminded me of the positive Christian roots of forgiveness that I had neglected in my effort to critique my own tradition. For that I am deeply indebted.

*Healing Without Forgiving* would not be what it is today were it not for my wonderful editor, Sarah Chauncey, who is tough but right on target. Even the most difficult feedback that I didn't initially agree with turned out to be exactly right and is represented in this final form. Thank you, Sarah! And to my artist and illustrator, Gwen Vogel—hats off! You have brought my pages alive with your graceful line drawings that represent the many survivors who are on a hero's journey. I can't forget John Koehler and his team at Koehler Books—Hannah, Lauren, and Adrienne—who managed final editing, design, and logistics to produce the beautiful product put before you now—thank you!

Finally, I thank my faithful husband, Ron, who never doubted I would complete this book and gave me feedback and encouragement each time it was needed. You are my rock!

Throughout the writing of this workbook, I kept asking myself why I was writing it. Why was it important for me to explore the concept of forgiveness in its many forms—forgiving self, forgiving friends, forgiving perpetrators? To this day, I don't have a ready answer. I only know I was driven to unearth the topic and give it air, and through the writing, learn what I believe. I do know that whether a dissociative survivor chooses to forgive or chooses not to forgive, they are on an arduous journey of healing that's embarked upon by heroes who trust—amid the pain, chaos, and confusion—that there's a better future ahead. Indeed, there IS a better future, and that's the good news that undergirds *Healing Without Forgiving: A Hero's Journey for Dissociative Survivors.*

Finally, praise and thanks to the One who heals regardless of the words we use!

# FOREWORD

*Do I have to forgive in order to heal?*

Therapy participants will commonly ask this question of their therapists; I've certainly heard it many times in my twenty-plus career as a clinical counselor. The conservative Christian background in which I was raised indoctrinated me in a very narrow version of forgiveness—a radical practice of forgiving, and indeed forgetting, no matter what for the sake of keeping the peace. I would later come to see this practice for what it really is: a convenient theology that lets those who perpetrate abuse off the hook. If the people that they wronged could not forgive, how easy it then is to point the finger of blame at *those people* and declare them as the wrong or sinful ones for not having a forgiving spirit.

I applaud Lyn Barrett for taking on such a heavy topic—forgiveness and its role in the healing process—in her latest book. When she asked me (as the Unicorn System, our collective's name) to share my/our story for the book, we jumped at the chance. We, a dissociative system, have a long and complicated relationship with forgiveness due to the spiritual abuse within high-demand religion that we experienced as a child. While we are not opposed to the practice of forgiveness and have come to a place of forgiveness as we define it, we also spent many years saying that we forgave those who wronged us, simply because it was the "Christian thing to do." Yet underneath that superficiality, or what we call "lip service" forgiveness in our story, there still existed a world of pain that needed to be named and shared. You will read more on that in the pages that follow.

In my role as a professional therapist, trauma educator, and author, my interest in the topic that Lyn tackles in this book goes beyond my personal story. Because I believe that whether to forgive, not to forgive, or to work with some other word or concept (like acceptance) that fits better than forgiveness is a personal decision that must be made by the person (or their system). There is no one right way to heal. And many people in the therapy, wellness, and spiritual/religious industries seem to work overtime these days on being the healing police of what constitutes real or deep healing and what doesn't. No one can determine this for you. I believe that it is a major truth that Lyn Barrett uses to guide what she shares and how she shares it in this book.

May you find what you are looking for in these pages as you embark on or continue with your own hero's journey to explore healing as you will define it.

**Jamie Marich, PhD**
Author of *Dissociation Made Simple: A Stigma-Free Guide to Embracing Your Dissociative Mind and Navigating Life*
Akron, Ohio
May 2025

# INTRODUCTION

As a survivor of chronic childhood trauma who was diagnosed with dissociative identity disorder (DID) in 1992, I bring **good news**.

Your wounds have made life difficult and disorienting today, but healing will make you wise and whole tomorrow. You may feel confused and fearful now, but clarity and security are over the horizon. You are not relegated to a half life limited by pain and doom, but to a whole life marked by joy, sorrow, happiness, sadness, achievement, failure, and all other human emotions and experiences. Because you were resourceful enough to survive then, you are resourceful enough to heal now. You are not the speck of dust on the floor that some of your parts may believe. You are—all of you—the bright, creative, worthy person who has embarked on a journey to discover yourself.

The **good news** is you're alive.

The **good news** is you have the capacity to thrive.

The **good news** is you can imagine a future.

The **good news** is you can become whole.

You are the hero of your story and, as such, you have the power to transform yourself both inwardly and outwardly to become the person you're meant to be. Don't get me wrong. Healing isn't easy; in fact, it's difficult beyond belief. But the very fact that you're here with this workbook means you have the drive to heal from horrible, unimaginable abuse.

*Healing Without Forgiving: A Hero's Journey for Dissociative Survivors* is meant to be a guide—one of many—for you on this journey. Other guides include your compassionate, trauma-informed therapist, your friends and family members who have proven themselves trustworthy, your own forged-in-the-fire intuition, and the work of healing that's described in this workbook.

Like it or not, you have picked up the mantle, and you're crossing the threshold as we speak. Mentors and companions will cross your path. Trials and obstacles will impede your progress. All the while, you'll go inward to find the grit to continue in the face of impossible pain.

One obstacle you may face is the false assumption that forgiving is a moral high ground in the healing landscape, and that forgiving your perpetrator is a requirement for healing. From an alternative perspective, *Healing Without Forgiving* will look at healing as the greater process, with forgiving as one option in the healing universe. Forgiveness is a tiny slice of restoring your emotional, mental, and physical health; healing is the whole pie. Forgiveness may be one objective out of a hundred; healing is the overarching goal that opens up new life, new insights, and new possibilities. Many survivors find wholeness through the healing journey, but few find forgiveness as the path to healing. Instead, healing is the path to forgiving, if that is a desired outcome.

A hero's journey has a reward at the end, like the treasure at the end of the rainbow. All your hard work will not be for naught. On the contrary, you will fulfill your intention to heal and live into your vision for wholeness. For you, and all of us who have experienced chronic childhood trauma, the reward you will receive is a happy, healthy life. Ultimately, *that* is the **good news** you're waiting to hear!

## WHAT IS DISSOCIATION?

*Healing Without Forgiving* is meant for people who've been chronically abused as children and want to heal from those experiences to live the life they were meant to live.

Whether you're diagnosed with a dissociative disorder or not, if you've been abused as a child, you probably use dissociation as one of your coping strategies. In its simplest sense, dissociation is the temporary separation of body and mind. The mind goes one place while the body is in another place. Typical signs of dissociation include spacing out, disappearing from what you consider your current life, or feeling a sense of unreality.[1] Dissociation is also manifest in cordoning off thoughts, feelings, and memories into different compartments in the mind, resulting in multiple "parts" or "alters."

In this workbook, I use the words "parts" and "insiders" when referring to the parts of our brains that were created through dissociation. The names we give to our parts may be personal and intimate; please feel free to translate into whatever words or phrases that are meaningful for you.

My focus on parts comes from my own diagnosis and the diagnoses of many of my peers. You may have experienced childhood abuse and you may feel spacey at times, but the concept of parts may not resonate with you. If this topic feels right otherwise, I encourage you to stick with us anyway and translate parts language into whatever metaphors work for you. Explore the world of parts through other sources such as *The Inner Child Workbook*[2] and *The Internal Family Systems Workbook.*[3]

With or without parts, if you experienced childhood abuse or other traumatic wounds, if you dissociate as a coping strategy, and if you're on a healing journey, then this workbook is for you.

## WHAT TO EXPECT

Using the metaphor of the hero's journey, we'll explore what's up ahead so you can prepare yourself for your voyage.

In chapter 1, "The Beginning," you'll set a healing intention and learn how forgiving fits within the larger context of healing.

In chapter 2, "A False Start," you'll discover that forgiving perpetrators, for most people, is a distraction from the hard work of healing. This chapter is packed with information about the challenges associated with forgiving perpetrators; if you find it overwhelming, feel free to jump forward and, as you're ready, go back and read it in small doses.

In chapter 3, "The Initiation," you'll discover how to forgive yourself and take some steps to get there.

In chapter 4, "Companions," you'll explore relationship triggers and how healing them enables you to find trustworthy people to journey with you.

In chapter 5, "The Threshold," you'll learn about the importance of a therapist and the establishment of safety and stability.

In chapter 6, "The Quest," you'll navigate the Healing Wheel that uncovers the work that will heal your wounds.

In chapter 7, "Many Rewards," you'll discover the surprise benefits you reap when you heal.

In chapter 8, "Coming Home," you'll claim your ultimate reward: a happy, healthy life, even as you continue your journey.

Throughout the workbook, you'll find questions that will invite you to think about your journey and spaces for you to journal the questions. Some people express themselves best through writing and may need to add additional pages to the exercises provided. Others express themselves better in art mediums, music, or other forms of expression. Please feel free to explore the questions in your own chosen medium with as much or as little detail as you like. And for those who enjoy coloring as creative expression, feel free to color the illustrations in this workbook in whatever way is pleasing to you.

## PACE YOURSELF

All journeys take time, and the hero's journey is no exception. In fact, given the challenges the hero faces, the journey becomes a lifelong quest. Take your time. Give yourself space to heal if triggers arise. This workbook encompasses decades of work, so there's no rush. You are preparing for a marathon, not a sprint, so pace yourself.

## THE QUEST FOR WHOLENESS

A voice deep inside calls you to a healing journey, beginning today. You may question whether you're up to the task, but let me assure you, you are. There are mountains to climb, rivers to forge, companions to meet, and dragons to slay—all very specific to you. You are the only one who can tame this landscape. You can do it, and you will do it, one step at a time. Bon voyage!

# 1

# THE BEGINNING

*Every story starts somewhere.*

Gabby was sitting in a little Zoom box on my desktop screen along with twelve other people who attended the first gathering of writers who had been diagnosed with a dissociative disorder. Her neatly trimmed dark-brown hair and her steady eyes gave her a serious, attentive look. I would learn, over time, that she was committed to the writing process as a form of healing. Gabby would become a loyal soldier in our evolving group, which would later be named Dissociative Writers, and she would take on roles that would help the group grow into a nonprofit. On that particular day, though, we began a friendship between two broken but resilient people who were determined to become whole.

As friends do, we had lots of conversations, and one of them was about healing. "My ultimate healing intention is to function in the world as an integrated person," Gabby told me several years into our friendship. "My whole being will know, accept, and feel my entire life narrative without needing to resort to dissociation or self-injury to cope."

Gabby was reflecting on what a *whole life* might look like for her, and she went on to build a beautiful vision of healing with detail, depth, and scope. Her body, mind, and spirit knew where she wanted to go; now her task was getting there.

Curious about how forgiving her perpetrators might play into her healing, I asked Gabby about the popular wisdom that to heal you must forgive.

"Forgiving my perpetrators has never even been on my radar," she replied. "I've been too consumed with simply surviving and healing to even consider my perps." As a survivor of chronic childhood abuse and a diagnosis of dissociative identity disorder, Gabby went on to add that healing, for her, was far more important than forgiving.

> *"The gold star of trauma recovery is healing, with or without forgiving."*

Gabby's response to forgiving her perpetrators is similar to the response of many of us with severe trauma in our backgrounds. Forgiveness is out of sight, out of mind, and the work of healing is all-consuming. By the same token, her willingness to set an intention for healing is life-giving. As she envisions what a whole life will look like for her, she is setting an internal compass that will lead her in that direction, even when life is difficult, and she makes no conscious effort to access her intention. Healing, not forgiving, is the force that drives her forward, the magnetic attraction that keeps her going.

The gold star of trauma recovery is healing, with or without forgiving. One way of describing healing is "a holistic, transformative process of repair and recovery in mind, body, and spirit resulting in positive change, finding meaning, and movement toward self-realization of wholeness, regardless of the presence or absence of disease."[4]

The work of healing chronic childhood trauma is intense and ongoing, but positive change, meaning, and wholeness are possible. You may find yourself getting to know your parts, dealing with overpowering triggers, planning for your future, healing relationships, and struggling with memory recall all at the same time. Later in this workbook, we'll explore the Healing Wheel, which sets the path for your work ahead. But for now, the important thing to remember is that healing involves a whole host of interrelated tasks that will both confound you and energize you. Healing from trauma—as a transformative process of repair and recovery in mind, body, and spirit—is not for the faint of heart. But it is very doable for a survivor like you.

Whew! Does healing sound overwhelming? You're right, and that's why it's important to set your healing intention.

## SETTING A HEALING INTENTION

You may have heard the old adage, "You can't see the forest for the trees." In the midst of recovery from chronic childhood trauma, it may be difficult, at times, to see where you're going while trees, bushes, and undergrowth pop up all over the place. Setting a healing intention, then, is your compass for navigating the trees and undergrowth. The forest you're heading toward is a happy, healthy, whole life.

Gabby set an intention by visualizing or imagining what life would look like on the other side of deep healing. Her healing intention helps her steer her course when she's overwhelmed with fear, doom, inner chaos, and memories. In times like this, her intention may be on the back burner and her steering may be unconscious, but some part within her knows the direction, follows the blueprint she's already set, and moves her toward her hopes and dreams, step by step.

Like Gabby, Sarah was diagnosed with dissociative identity disorder. When she imagines herself healed and whole, she sees all parts of herself pulling together in the same direction with the same general goals instead of in conflict with one another. She wants to be in the here and now for the vast majority of the time, rather than reliving memories or lurking in her past. For Sarah, healthy relationships mean that they're not contaminated by her history but, rather, grounded in her present. Forgiving her perpetrators has never been a part of Sarah's healing intention, yet even without forgiving, she can imagine a better future than she's living today.

Barbie was another participant in the same writing group Gabby attended. Initially, she was tentative and uncertain about using her voice, but, over time, she's discovered that her voice is important and valid. Her healing intention is to recognize her own significance in God's eyes, to know her worth, and to live into her true potential. She wants to be able to feel without drowning. She's noticed that she tends toward black-and-white thinking, which she finds limiting, and she would like to appreciate nuance. Since Barbie's faith is important to her, she believes forgiving her perpetrators is a critical part of her Christian journey and includes that in her healing intention.

I was first introduced to healing intentions by my friend and colleague Linda Crockett,[5] who was coaching me through a difficult time several decades ago. Linda invited me to set an intention for our work together, and through this work I learned that an intention reflects the underlying purpose that motivates me. While working with Linda, I embodied my intention successfully and moved forward in a specific area of my life.

Interestingly, as I was writing my memoir, *Crazy: Reclaiming Life from the Shadow of Traumatic Memory*,[6] I found a passage in an old journal that I incorporated into the manuscript. Long before I ever heard about intentions, I discovered I had set one for myself as I was deep into my difficult healing journey:

> I never wanted to be crazy. Almost from the beginning of my decompensation, when I had the energy to think about it, I wanted to be sane and normal, with a shot at happiness, just like other people. For me, that meant that I would resume life without a myriad of voices, without an endless stream of pain, without feeling like a victim, without the sense of unreality that so often enveloped me. Instead, my sense of self would be unified and integrated, my bonds with my real children would be renewed, I would have a loving relationship with another human being, and I would no longer be a victim. I would be a survivor, a thriver. I would own my own power and leave my pervasive sense of powerlessness behind.[7]

I never considered forgiving my perpetrators to be an important part of my healing. I have, however, sought a sense of peace and resolution to my pain. Acceptance of what happened might be a better way to describe my relationship to my now-deceased perpetrators. And a relentless pursuit to create a better life for myself and those I love.

How do you imagine yourself healed and whole? What is your intention for healing?

## EXERCISE 1: SETTING YOUR HEALING INTENTION

**Each of us carries dreams about what our life will look like in the future. For those of us who have experienced childhood trauma, that will inevitably include healing. Set your intention for healing. What does healing look like to you? Write a description of your hopes and dreams for your future self that reflect your values, your desires, and how you hope to get there.**

## WHAT IS FORGIVING AND HOW DOES IT FIT?

With your healing intention readily in hand, you can look at forgiveness, create your own definition, and discover how it fits into the universe of healing using this workbook and your own best wisdom.

I would love to give you a firm definition of forgiveness, but I can't. In spite of the fact that forgiveness is promoted by world religions, psychological research, and secular culture, there's no consensus on what it means.

At the very least, forgiveness is *the act of releasing the pain caused by another person.*

Still, questions pop up over which there is little agreement. Is forgiveness a reciprocal act between the offended and offender, meaning the offender participates in righting the wrong? Or is forgiveness the solo act of the offended, driven perhaps by religious beliefs or a desire to let go of the pain? Is forgiveness an emotion or an action, or is it both? Does forgiveness require us to feel compassion and generosity toward our offender, or is neutrality an acceptable end result? Is forgiveness a one-and-done decision, or is it a process that takes time to live into? Is forgiving a perpetrator who committed crimes different from forgiving yourself or forgiving a faithful friend? Are some offenses too heinous to forgive? We will look more carefully at some of these questions in the chapters to come.

Although some would have you believe that forgiveness is the path to healing, healing is, in fact, the container within which forgiving may or may not occur. Releasing the pain of hurt does not always accompany forgiving; in fact, forgiving prematurely may increase the pain. On the other hand, releasing the pain of hurt always accompanies the in-depth work of healing. If you want to let go of your pain, engaging in the arduous work of healing is your top priority.

As one thread in the larger tapestry of healing, forgiving in some contexts is critical to your growth. For instance, forgiving yourself enables you to see yourself from a perspective that's different from the perspective that was imposed upon you since your youth. Forgiving yourself means you are learning to love yourself.

By the same token, learning which of your friends and family members are trustworthy and deserve your forgiveness when they inadvertently hurt you enables you to work through your triggers and grow in healthy relationships. Forgiving trustworthy friends and family members roots you in a community that can support you on your healing journey.

> *"Although some would have you believe that forgiveness is the path to healing, healing is, in fact, the container within which forgiving may or may not occur."*

Again, these acts of forgiving are woven into your healing process and make you stronger, wiser, and more ready to engage in friendships, intimacy, and authentic communication.

How would you define forgiveness and what role does it play in your healing journey?

## EXERCISE 2: HOW DO YOU DEFINE FORGIVENESS?

**In the space below, write your own definition of forgiveness. Try to let go of what you've been taught in your faith community, in school, by your family, and in other venues. Use some of the questions I've posed above to explore the concept of forgiveness in a way that makes sense to you. Is forgiveness a part of your healing journey? Why or why not?**

## THE HERO'S JOURNEY

Joseph Campbell, an author best known for his work with Bill Moyers and the TV series *The Power of Myth*,[8] articulated the archetypal hero's journey found in stories throughout the ages. In my experience, we are all given the opportunity to take that journey that calls us to achieve a greater purpose. If we accept the challenge, we leave home and encounter many obstacles along the way. Sometimes our journey is smooth sailing, but other times our very lives are at stake. The hero keeps moving forward in spite of the daunting difficulties, never knowing what lies ahead or whether or not the purpose will be achieved. After slaying a dragon or two, discovering companions, and picking up wisdom here and there, the hero discovers themself back home with more than when they began. As T. S. Eliot, the American poet and playwright, wrote:

*We shall not cease from exploration*
*And the end of all our exploring*
*Will be to arrive where we started*
*And know the place for the first time.*[9]

The moral of every hero's journey is that when we grapple with the trials put before us, we are transformed. We see what was already there, though hidden from our view, as if we are seeing it for the first time. Like Dorothy in *The Wizard of Oz*, we survive life-threatening adventures to come home to the place where we started and understand it with new eyes.

I cannot imagine a more apt way to describe the healing journey of people who have experienced chronic childhood trauma. You and I are heroes. We may each define our purpose differently, but, however we define it, it compels us to move forward through impossible challenges so that we will know ourselves, our history, our present, and our future in ways deeper than we could have imagined when we began.

Are you ready? Dragons need slaying. Moats need crossing. Unknown friends are waiting for you. Your healing intention is pointing you toward your destination and your quest calls.

But first, let's look at a survivor's story. (You'll find one at the end of each chapter.) Then, before taking your first step, we'll explore how forgiving perpetrators could be an unnecessary obstacle on your journey.

## SURITA'S STORY

When Surita was a little girl, she loved school. It was safe, and the teacher was nice. She needed a lot of remedial help, but still, Surita thought she'd like to be a teacher when she grew up. In her child's heart, she would grow up to teach children like herself so they would never have to feel "less than"—the way she felt. Indeed, Surita did grow up to be a teacher, and for forty-four years she taught school, mostly kindergarten, achieving the goal she had set for herself.

Surita has a natural gift for the arts. As a high schooler, she began to play guitar and formed a trio with friends, where she both wrote and performed music. In college, she took ballet lessons along with children and other adults. Surita joined a ballet company in adulthood and has continued informal dance throughout her life. She dabbled in art as a part of her healing journey and recently published her memoir, *Quilted: Piecing Together My Dissociated Selves*.[10]

Surita came from a dysfunctional family where her father abused his wife and all three children, although Surita got the worst of it. Her mother was unable to protect the family from her husband's volatility, and neither parent was able to provide role models for positive relationships. Surita was "Daddy's little girl" and, in the words of one of her Littles, "I got two daddies. A good daddy and a bad daddy. I love my good daddy."

When Surita was thirty years old, her internal life began to disintegrate after a relationship breakup. The abusive relationship mimicked her upbringing where Surita was engulfed by her partner's wants and need. Therapy helped her maintain her professional life, but her personal life was in shambles. When she turned forty, she was diagnosed with dissociative identity disorder and began the long and arduous task of meeting her alters, facilitating communication, working through body memories, and more. Over the years, Surita's name changed to the author name she uses today: Suritaplus.

"To me, the word *forgiveness* feels scratchy," she says. "I hear it as a judgment: If I don't forgive, it means I'm a bad person, I'm not able to heal, or I 'should just get over it' because that's the right way to 'move on.' I think those who want to tell others that forgiveness is necessary in order to heal might be better received if they offer forgiveness as, not the only one, but one of many possible paths to healing."

At the age of seventy-four, Surita continues to work on her healing. She has come to a place of peace with her history and has no need for closure with either her abuser or his enablers. "I think I'm a therapy-lifer and probably always will be." Before her father died, Surita confronted him, but she had to work with her alters about the confrontation first, to give each a chance to weigh in about their feelings. She says she has compassion for her father as a boy, who experienced his own terrible abuse, but not for him as an adult, who made choices that harmed her and others. Surita continues to get in touch with her anger over her inability to maintain a healthy, nurturing relationship—the legacy of her chronic childhood abuse.

"If he had asked for forgiveness, I would have asked him why he deserved it," Surita says. "Whether his answer was a true apology reflecting a genuine understanding of our situation or not, I would not forgive him. I have genuine compassion for the child he was, but I have no compassion for the abuser he became to his own wife and children."

# 2

# A FALSE START

*Forgiving perpetrators is a distraction from the quest.*

Not long ago, I was researching the topic of forgiveness for a conference-presentation proposal and a potential journal article. I read sermons, scientific articles, and the words of great thinkers to mine the meaning of the word. I discovered that no one had come to agreement on a definition. Nonetheless, with a few exceptions, most experts proclaimed that forgiveness was attainable, provided mental and physical health benefits, and could be integrated into therapeutic modalities for the benefit of the client. A large body of literature encouraged therapists to help the client set forgiveness as a goal. I closed my books and shuffled out to our patio, where my husband Ron and I would have happy hour before dinner.

"You're looking pretty serious about something," Ron observed as he watched me sip my wine. I told him about my research but reflected that something wasn't sitting right with me. I knew that forgiveness could release bitterness and resentment and allow the forgiver to let go of past wounds and move forward. I knew that my healing journey had led me right up to the door of forgiveness, and had maybe even opened it. I knew I was a happy and fulfilled person and wasn't aware of any bitterness poisoning my life.

"I love science, Ron, and I love scientists." I grinned at the retired scientist I had married. "But scientists can be very cold and dispassionate when they're talking about"—my body began to shake—"something they know nothingthefuck about"—the tears began to flow—"and they think they know whatthefuck is good for me"—I was now heaving and gasping for air—"and I hate the word forgiveness and I shouldn't have to use it just because a bunch of fuckingmaleresearchers think it's a fuckinggood word"—my face contorted and my breath eluded me—"and I shouldn't have to set a goal to achieve it just because goals are fuckingmeasurable and those samefuckingmaleresearchers want good fuckingresearchresults."

It took me ten minutes to gather in my tears. "By setting goals, they're taking my agency thefuck away from me and they don't have the fuckingright to do that." It would take the rest of the evening to feel the angst dissipate and normalcy settle in. Mike, my alter who holds my anger, was hiding obediently for years among the folds of my neurons. He woke up abruptly with something to say.

Ron got up to throw the hamburgers on the grill but made a detour behind my chair. He put his hands on my shoulders and rubbed them gently. And I cried some more.

## DO I HAVE TO FORGIVE MY PERPETRATORS?

Although we'll talk about some reasons you'll want to learn how to forgive in future chapters, assuming you have to forgive your perpetrators is a false start. You have a choice that depends on many variables. Your culture, your religion, your family, and the way you define forgiveness will impact how you approach forgiving the people responsible for your wounds. Forgiveness, after all, keeps the focus on them and not on you. The perpetrators who had power over you then, have power over you now, by virtue of any desire to forgive. Embarking on a forgiveness process invites them into your consciousness when you most need your body, mind, and spirit to be fully available for your own needs.

Healing without regard to forgiving relegates your perpetrator to the background and makes space for you to work on you. There was a time when their presence loomed over every part of you, even if they were out of your life, even if they were dead. As you heal, you can bring them forward when you need to, but you can also put them in a box on the shelf in your closet or some other safe compartment you create. When they're tucked neatly away and no longer hovering over your every move, you'll be amazed at how much internal space you've freed up.

Yes, they're still there. Yes, they impacted your life in terrible ways. Yes, they're scuttling around in that box trying to get out. But as you heal, their power will diminish, and someday you'll discover that they've lost their ability to trigger you, or all the wind has gone out of their sails, or maybe they've even disappeared from the box that you once kept under lock and key. You no longer need them, and you no longer need the box, not because you've forgiven them but because you've healed.

Anastasia Pollock, LCMHC, frames the issue of forgiveness this way:

> I work with people who have experienced horrific traumas at the hands of other people. These traumas include acts of sexual abuse, rape, exploitation, and physical and emotional abuse. Some of the perpetrators are relatives and some are not. Regardless, the degree of trauma in each of these cases is significant and has had a major impact on their lives and well-being. The people I work with in the therapy room are resilient and courageous. They are able to work through their traumas, but many get caught up on one point: They believe they are supposed to forgive the perpetrator but can't seem to get there. This is what I tell them: You don't have to forgive in order to move on.[11]

The answer to the question posed above, then, is, "No. You don't have to forgive your perpetrators in order to heal." Let's explore some of the issues that complicate forgiving perpetrators so we can set aside the false start and begin the journey anew.

## INTERNAL PRESSURE

The greatest pressure we face to forgive comes from within. We are basically good people. We want to do right at the same time we're healing from wrong. We live in a society that highly values forgiveness, and we're inundated by its benefits everywhere we turn.

As small children on the playground, we remember being told to apologize if we hurt someone and to accept that apology if it was given to us. Whether or not that exchange was sincere and effective, we walked away from the altercation knowing that forgiving was a part of adult expectations, though not necessarily meant to resolve the issues in authentic ways.

If we are people of faith, we probably hear about forgiving every time we gather with our faith community. Even if we are not religious, we may be inundated with mindfulness wisdom that promotes forgiveness as a way to achieve wholeness and peace. Even social media surrounds us with a gauzy image of the forgiveness imperative.

For instance, a quick look at recent Facebook posts shows some typical ideas about forgiveness:

> *Holding a grudge doesn't make you strong, it makes you bitter. Forgiveness doesn't make you weak, it sets you free.*
>
> *There's nothing more classy or powerful than showing forgiveness and grace to someone who doesn't deserve it.*
>
> *Forgive others, not because they deserve forgiveness, but because you deserve peace.*

Mother Teresa tells us: "If we really want to love, we must learn how to forgive." Mahatma Gandhi tells us: "The weak can never forgive. Forgiveness is the attribute of the strong." Martin Luther King Jr. tells us: "Forgiveness is not an occasional act; it is a constant attitude." Desmond Tutu tells us: "There is nothing that cannot be forgiven, and there is no one undeserving of forgiveness."

In these few brief words, our wisdom teachers have captured beautiful, but often unattainable, images of the power of forgiveness without referring to what forgiveness means to them, who is involved in the forgiveness process, or whether some acts of violence require healing before or in place of forgiving.

> *"The greatest pressure we face to forgive comes from within."*

The upshot for you and me is that without one person suggesting, let alone pressuring, us to forgive our perpetrators, we are already conditioned to do so. We're inspired by our Facebook feed. We're informed by our childhood experiences. We're motivated by famous people who tell us stories about forgiving. We're held in check by our faith communities who suggest divine displeasure if we don't forgive. To forgive is an imperative that's in our social genes, even when it leads to our destruction.

## EXERCISE 3: SOCIAL MESSAGES ABOUT FORGIVENESS

**Have you internalized any social messages that encourage you to forgive your perpetrators? If so, do you know what they are? Write them below, if you are able. Do you know where they come from? (Please note that sometimes we're not even aware of the origin of our internal beliefs.)**

## RELIGIOUS PRESSURE

I am a Christian. I was raised by atheists but found God when my wounds left me hopeless and helpless. Because my newfound faith was also a lifesaver, I went to seminary and became an ordained minister as part of my healing journey. I served several churches and led many prayers and liturgies that called on the congregation to forgive the trespassers in their lives.

During my church ministry, a prayer community became a second home to me, where people—other ordained clergy, religious, and lay people—could share what was going on in their lives. Processing my new calling as well as the residue of my trauma-informed life with these special people was a gift. They supported me and loved me. They were nonjudgmental. I trusted them. They were safe. So I knew it came out of love when a couple put a book about forgiveness into my hands.

"You've told us about the horrors you've had to endure. Maybe it's time you forgive your perpetrators as a part of your walk with God." I looked at the book and turned it around this way and that. It was small, but it felt heavy. My eyesight was good, but the words blurred in response to this gift. It might as well have been a strange document in a foreign tongue. I'm sure they thought this book would help me on my journey. Instead, it stopped me in my tracks. It felt like pressure to forgive, and I wasn't interested.

Religion has a lot to say about forgiveness. Every major world religion suggests that forgiveness is a quality we should cultivate and strive for, although each religion has a slightly different understanding of the concept. Judaism, Islam, and Christianity—called the three Abrahamic religions because they all descend from Abraham and Sarah—are cases in point. Among them, Islam encourages forgiveness, Judaism says forgiveness is necessary only if the offender repents and attempts to make amends, but only Christianity embraces forgiveness as the path to salvation.

Although common Christian wisdom teaches that Jesus's words on forgiveness are a call to forgive regardless of the participation or lack of participation of the offender, recent interpretations by biblical scholars Maria Mayo[12] and Susannah Griffith[13] say differently. Indeed, both demonstrate that Jesus in the Gospels expects repentance before forgiveness, largely for the sake of reuniting the community. I explore these Christian interpretations a bit more in appendix A.

Some Christian survivors tell of the deep struggle they've engaged in to come to a place of forgiveness, and, with faith and perseverance, they were successful. In my case, the religious pressure I felt to forgive was benign and grew out of love. In many situations, however, religion can put strict rules around forgiveness and retraumatize victims by expecting them to shoulder the work of forgiving as they watch the perpetrator go scot-free, all while they're trying to heal from wounds inflicted by that perpetrator.

Some of this is related to insulated, patriarchal religions that expect the woman to obey her husband under any circumstance. In extreme cases, she is cast out of the community if she refuses to do so. Pressure to forgive in situations such as this is another form of abuse that produces layer upon layer of distorted and destructive wounds, falsely in the name of God.

Religion not only pressures victims to forgive, it may also comfort victims with the authentic promise of God's grace. For those whose faith is instrumental to their healing, it's important to discern with trustworthy people how God is working within them to bring them to wholeness.

## EXERCISE 4: RELIGIOUS MESSAGES ABOUT FORGIVENESS

**If you participate in a faith tradition, can you name its beliefs about forgiveness? Do you find this helpful or harmful? Is your faith community supportive of your healing process?**

**If you are not a part of a faith community, do you have spiritual views that relate to forgiving perpetrators? Do you have a secular community that supports you in this?**

## PSYCHOLOGICAL PRESSURE

It's hard to know whether religion influenced researchers or researchers influenced religion, but the call to forgive as a unilateral responsibility of the victim only has become a groundswell in both the house of worship and academia. Not to mention, of course, the popular media which often draws its messages from those two sources.

A large segment of the psychological research community supports the notion that forgiving someone who harms you is good for your health, and, indeed, there's plenty of evidence to support this claim. Robert Enright and Fred Luskin both lead large research teams to study the effects of forgiveness on mental health. Enright, and colleague Suzanne R. Friedman, cite forgiveness as a goal for incest survivors in a 1996 study.[14] Luskin says we create a "grievance story" which, he notes is our "enemy," as a part of our "endless stories of victimization."[15]

Both men, and other researchers in their field, are attempting to do good by encouraging forgiveness for the general population, which may differ in impact from survivors of chronic childhood abuse. Both have written popularized books that are available in your favorite bookstore. Neither disclaim their approaches to forgiveness as not applicable to some populations such as survivors of chronic childhood abuse.

Fortunately, many clinicians have a more nuanced understanding of the healing landscape for survivors of childhood abuse. Trauma-informed therapists understand that healing is a lengthy process that may or may not culminate in forgiving perpetrators. They provide a container within which their clients can do the extensive work of healing without pressuring or even suggesting that forgiveness should be a goal.

> *"Trauma-informed therapists understand that healing is a lengthy process that may or may not culminate in forgiving perpetrators."*

For instance, psychologist Jeanne M. Slattery suggests that forgiveness can be a positive experience when a person is given the freedom to choose, while pressuring them to forgive can be retraumatizing. Women are often accused of being bitter and their feelings and experiences questioned when they express justifiable anger, she says. Forced forgiveness tends to turn that anger into shame and reinforce a survivor's sense of powerlessness. Rather than helping the person heal, forgiveness "seems to be used to reduce the discomfort of the perpetrator or the perpetrator's friends and family—at the victim's expense."[16]

Judie is a Christian who leads groups for therapists and survivors of ritual abuse and mind control. Bright and articulate, she describes the pressure she continues to feel as she heals:

> *I feel pressure from people who are into thinking positive about everything. They can be Christians, or not. Many people of many beliefs are that way. "Keep a positive attitude. Forgive or you won't be forgiven." My own personal forgiveness is not contingent upon forgiving perpetrators like my father. My own personal forgiveness is between me and God, contingent upon my own repentance and my own faith in Christ . . . I do know that trying to smooth life over by getting everyone "to just love everyone" is a gross cover-up of reality and a lie, deceiving themselves into thinking that forgiveness will solve the world's problems. Between being told, "Can't you just forgive and be happy?" or "Forgive or you won't be forgiven," it really sends me running from the subject!*

Judie believes the pressure to forgive often comes from our discomfort with the reality of the abuse that we endured. Instead of saying, "I'm sorry for your suffering," and showing us compassion, people demand survivors to forgive as their way of handling unspeakable truths, in her experience. "Most people don't know how to relate to us," she says, "so they immediately jump to forgiveness."

## EXERCISE 5: OTHER MESSAGES ABOUT FORGIVENESS

**Has pressure from others to forgive your abusers played a part in your healing process? Invite your parts into a dialogue below where they share honestly about any pressure they've felt to forgive.**

## MULTIPLE PERSPECTIVES

As a person on the dissociative spectrum, you probably have more than one part and, therefore, more than one perspective. Forgiving the people who are responsible for your fragmented mind is complicated. Each part may have different concerns about the various matters that impact such a decision. For instance, one part may love a perpetrator with all their heart and have already offered forgiveness in the desire to maintain that bond. Another may try to hide from the issue and ignore any steps you take toward reconciliation. Another may be angry at the world in general and try to sabotage any gains you make in healing. Another may want to obliterate your perpetrators and kill them on sight. You may hold within you abandoned infants, terrified small children, rebellious teenagers, and vigilant protectors who need a voice in your healing process and, by extension, any act of forgiveness you are considering.

*"As a person on the dissociative spectrum, you probably have more than one part and, therefore, more than one perspective."*

Each internal part needs to heal, and that process will look different and take different amounts of time for each. The host (or predominantly front-facing alter) may be cool with forgiving, but not all parts may agree. Communication between your parts and within your system is critical for a healthy healing process.

Our friend Judie questions how anyone could expect an infant or small child to forgive before they understand what happened to them. Since we have very young parts, large aspects of us are incapable of forgiving even if other parts are ready to take that step. She reflects, here, on the impact of dissociative identities on the forgiveness process:

> *I believe no one can expect people with dissociated parts to forgive without healing first. A child must first understand why they were hurt before having the ability to forgive. Understanding is crucial to forgiving. Without it, forgiving means nothing. It can't happen. It is so very wrong to expect that of someone who is multiple, without helping them first understand why they were broken. Instead of saying, "A person must forgive in order to heal," it should be, "A person needs to heal before they can forgive." People get it backwards.*

You are one, but you are more than one. When you are contemplating forgiving someone who abused you, it's important to take it slowly. Asking inside what others have to say is a first step. Working with your therapist provides a critical reality check. Moving forward with forgiving your perpetrators is not a good idea until you have reached a true internal consensus with all your parts. If consensus isn't possible, continue your healing process knowing that forgiving isn't necessary.

## EXERCISE 6: ARE YOU READY?

**Ask inside whether you are ready to forgive your abusers. Specifically, check in with your preverbal parts (if you have any), your submissive parts, and your protector parts. Finally, let any other part(s) with thoughts about forgiving your perpetrators weigh in. Invite each part to write or draw their answer.**

## UNILATERAL VS. BILATERAL FORGIVENESS

*Unilateral forgiveness* means that only the victim, the survivor, or the person who was offended does the work of forgiving. Reams of writing attest that for some people forgiving, without the participation of the offender, is beneficial. In any case, unilateral forgiveness aims at transformation for one person only. *Bilateral forgiveness* means both the offended and the offender participate together in a process where the offender acknowledges, repents, and makes amends before forgiveness occurs. Bilateral forgiveness has biblical roots where the ultimate goal is transformation of both the individuals and the community. It's likely that bilateral forgiveness is more difficult to achieve as it requires deep self-reflection on the part of the person who committed the offense.

Today, psychological and religious experts place their emphasis on unilateral rather than bilateral forgiveness. It's for us, they say, not our perpetrators. While it's ideal to have the offender participate, it's not necessary because the exercise is for the wounded, not for the one who did the wounding. They remind us that forgiveness does not mean condoning the behavior, forgetting, minimizing our hurt, reconciling, or giving up our feelings.[17] Instead, they say forgiveness lifts a heavy burden from our backs and gives us freedom.

*"Today, psychological and religious experts place their emphasis on unilateral rather than bilateral forgiveness."*

Most definitions of forgiveness describe a state similar to the one Janis Abrahms Spring, author of *How Can I Forgive You? The Courage to Forgive, the Freedom Not To*,[18] describes as "acceptance," where the victim comes to terms with the past, lets it go, and moves forward when the offender is unwilling or unable to participate. Spring says that acceptance is the best we can hope for when the offender is not willing or able to participate in the "genuine forgiveness" process that she outlines in her book. For Spring, genuine forgiveness requires acknowledgment and making amends.

Other researchers ask much more of the offended by assuming that forgiveness occurs outside of repentance, hoping the victim's grace compels healing in the perpetrator, and encouraging the victim to cultivate positive feelings for the perpetrator. Indeed, Robert Enright, whom we met earlier in this chapter, even suggests that we give offenders a gift as a way to seal the past and move forward into the future.[19] In a convoluted sense, these approaches place an undue burden on the victim to help the perpetrator.

I can barely begin to pick apart the problems in this approach for people who have been chronically abused in childhood. Suffice it to say that, as we get healthy, we also claim our power to feel and do what we choose to feel and do. If forgiving, feeling positive toward, and giving gifts to the person who hurt us makes us feel unsafe and uncomfortable, then it's not a choice to make. Rather, we can choose to set boundaries for ourselves that keep us safe and comfortable. Gabby, whom we met in chapter 1, explains from her perspective:

> *I believe forgiveness, true forgiveness, has to be bilateral, especially if the goal is to mend relationships. The perpetrator, or the enabler, definitely needs to acknowledge the harm they did, feel real remorse, and make amends to the survivor. I also believe this rarely happens, especially by the perpetrator. But if it does, if the perpetrator or enabler can hold themselves fully accountable for their actions, forgiveness may help mend relationships.*

Diane Pomerantz, PhD, says:

> Forgiveness is a relational concept and has been throughout the ages. It implies that the Forgiver and the Forgiven take a journey TOGETHER to reach reconciliation. Throughout time, this transactional process had been a means to resolve debt and other interpersonal injuries. Whatever the injury, genuine forgiveness involves more than just one person. Therefore, it makes no logical sense to consider forgiveness unless both parties are involved in the transaction.[20]

Pomerantz notes that the cyclical nature of abusive behavior leaves the victim in a precarious position when they engage in unilateral forgiveness with an abuser who has not accepted responsibility for the abusive acts. When there's no remorse, the perpetrator may interpret forgiveness as permission to continue the abuse. The victim may be setting themselves up for continued pain from a person who has shown themselves to be untrustworthy.

Bilateral forgiveness is rare among people with dissociative disorders, but it happens occasionally. Some survivors have experienced deep healing when their abuser reached out apologizing and asking for forgiveness. Understandably, not everyone is able to accept that apology or trust the person who gave it. Listen to your gut, check in with your trauma-informed therapist, and do what feels right. You're not obligated to accept an apology or offer forgiveness if your internal messengers are telling you no. For some of us, now may be the first time in our lives that we've put ourselves first. There's nothing selfish in that. It's good self-care. The work of healing has many important areas to address. Forgiving your perpetrator comes later, if at all.

## EXERCISE 7: YOUR ABUSER'S READINESS

**Have your perpetrator(s) acknowledged and made amends for their abuse? If not, what is the likelihood that might happen? Would you prefer they apologize and make amends, or would you rather leave them behind? Why or why not?**

## FORGIVING TOO SOON

Michael is a librarian with otherwise specified dissociative disorder (OSDD) who specializes in collating research on trauma. At times, he has been on disability because of severe suicidal ideation. In his complicated childhood, his mother was the only person who showed him love, but she also abused him sexually, emotionally, and psychologically. His compassion for others is profound, and he "understands" why she did what she did. Just before she died, she told him she was sorry, and he responded, "I forgive you."

Michael is angry at the circumstances that produced mental illness and dysfunction in his family, but he can't get angry at the person who abused him. He knows that his rage should be directed toward his mother and others in his family, but, instead, he's turned it inward on himself, which is why he periodically descends into darkness and has the desire to take his life. Michael's faux forgiveness has prevented him from doing the deep work with other parts that might heal his rage and give him a new lease on life.

> *"Because our identities are fluid, we may have trouble knowing where we stop and the other person begins."*

People with dissociative disorders often have a lot of compassion for the suffering of other people. We also have difficulty setting boundaries. Because our identities are fluid, we may have trouble knowing where we stop and the other person begins. We are vulnerable to letting these factors undermine our vision of healing for ourselves.

Sharri, whom we will meet shortly, was forced by her perpetrators to have compassion for them. Because of this, she's had a long journey learning how to individuate and embrace her autonomy separate from her abusers. Initially, Sharri had more compassion for them than for herself. After deep work, which included feeling her rage, Sharri can once again feel compassion for her abusers, but never to her own detriment.

Not everyone who forgives prematurely becomes suicidal. Sometimes we just carry a heavy burden that saps our energy and prevents us from tackling the issues our system puts before us. Forgiving too soon can be a distraction strategy that allows us to put off the real work we need to do.

Janis Abrahms Spring, whom we met earlier in this chapter, talks about cheap forgiveness as a way of burying or denying the pain rather than resolving it. "Cheap forgiveness," she says, "bypasses the injury—as well as any possibility of developing a healthy relationship with yourself or with the offender."[21] Even when an authentic apology is offered, it takes time for the offended person to process their anger and accept the apology. In the case of chronic childhood abuse, that processing may take years, if it occurs at all. As we noted earlier, each part of ourselves needs to do the work of healing before any unified consensus toward forgiving can be reached.

According to David Bedrick, JD, those who write blogs, articles, books, and spiritual one-liners that pressure people to forgive before they're ready "not only dismiss the real pain many people suffer; they discourage intelligent analysis of the traumas many people and groups experience." He goes on:

> Further, the attitude behind these statements can shame people, making them think that something is wrong with going through a natural process of healing after injury or betrayal where forgiveness may not be the first (or second or third) step. The truth is that many people don't forgive because it is not time to forgive—and taking the time to proceed at their own pace can be empowering, intelligent, and worthy. Simply put, it is alarming how un-psychological many psychologists can be; forgiveness is not the best medicine for all people all the time.[22]

Taking a shortcut in the healing process almost never works. It backfires. We may find ourselves stuck in the same place over and over again or propelled back to "start" on the board game of life.

## EXERCISE 8: MAKING A TIMELINE

**Make a timeline of your healing journey. Begin with your earliest memories and end with the intention you wrote in chapter 1. Where does forgiving your abusers fit on this timeline, if at all?**

## IT'S MY FAULT

Forgiving people who hurt us is complicated for people with dissociative disorders. Each of our parts may have different experiences, thoughts, and feelings about the person who offended. Our internal responses may seem confusing and conflicted, which is a sure warning sign that our system isn't in agreement. It's quite possible that we were told to keep our abuse a secret. We may have been told that it was our fault because we were so pretty or so pliable or simply so available. We might have feared harm for ourselves or our families if we talked about what happened.

When we forgive before doing the deep work of healing, we run the risk of believing the abuse was our fault. Our younger alters may have already taken that responsibility, and forgiving only compounds it. When we forgive alone, without our abuser acknowledging, apologizing, and making amends, our younger alters may translate that into meaning, "I'm at fault. I caused it. That's why I need to forgive."

Surita, whom we've met, says this about taking responsibility for the abuse:

> *Decades of therapy have taught my adult self that I was only a child. Nothing about it was my fault. However, internally, my sixteen-year-old blamed the three-four-five-year-old because the little one liked being Daddy's little princess and wanted his attention and the things he gave her. Through years of therapy, the teenager began to understand. The Little was simply being a little girl who loved her daddy.*

It was not your fault. You were a child without power among the adults in your life. Don't assume responsibility for what is not yours to own. Give that responsibility back to the people who own it.

> *"When we forgive before doing the deep work of healing, we run the risk of believing the abuse was our fault."*

## EXERCISE 9: IT WAS NOT YOUR FAULT

**Write this positive affirmation below, as many times as you wish: *It was not my fault.* Let other parts of you answer back in agreement, explanation, or disagreement. End the page with the positive affirmation: *It was not my fault.***

## NEGATIVE EMOTIONS

Robert Enright, whom we met earlier in this chapter, says in the first chapter of his book:

> People who talk with me about forgiveness often say that their resentment was a way of keeping the one who hurt them in a kind of emotional prison. As long as they held onto the anger and bitterness, the other stayed in the jail cell. Over time they began to realize that it was they, themselves, who were imprisoned by the hatred and not the other person. Our hatred affects us emotionally more than it affects the one who hurt us.[23]

There is certainly some truth to his premise. We have all been in that position where we felt that we were in jail while the other person was out there enjoying life, suffering no repercussions for their crimes, and maybe even hurting others just like they hurt us. Maybe, for instance, your abuser is a well-loved figure in the community who revels in accolades, while you're still suffering from the secret sessions in his basement that continued for years. Life isn't fair, and we may have experienced—and still are experiencing—anger, resentment, and bitterness.

The problem is that forgiveness gurus tend to assume that there are only two choices when healing from trauma: descending into anger, bitterness, and resentment when we don't forgive, or finding freedom when we do forgive. This black-and-white thinking puts us into another prison where we can't fathom forgiving and sense it will negatively impact our healing, yet we're told that life-destroying emotions are the sentence we've been given for the crime of being a victim of abuse. I'm guessing the intention you wrote for your healing in chapter 1 didn't include anger, resentment, and bitterness!

Anger, resentment, and bitterness are not the only negative emotions associated with the forgiveness process. While they may be noted in people who haven't forgiven, survivors of chronic early-childhood trauma may experience depression, self-loathing, and shame when they do forgive.

Tanya, a middle-aged woman who was diagnosed with a dissociative disorder, didn't trust her ex-husband, who not only cheated on her but gaslit her continually and befriended her parents who were her childhood abusers. After many years of in-depth healing work, she decided she wanted to forgive him, even though he had never acknowledged his part in their destroyed marriage. After writing a brief letter apologizing for any of her actions that had caused him pain and offering forgiveness for his actions that had caused her pain, she set the letter aside. That night, she awoke with nightmares and a deep sense of doom. Although she had built a happy life for herself, this attempt at forgiving brought forth triggers, not freedom.

Too many forgiveness experts jump too quickly into encouraging their clients to make a decision to forgive under the guise of preventing negative emotions. They neglect to give survivors time to experience their righteous anger. Negative emotions are appropriate for the context in which they were created.

In fact, negative emotions can be a positive step that leads toward healing. When you were abused as a child, your power was taken away from you. Getting in touch with your honest anger is one way to reclaim it. With deep work, you don't need to get stuck in bitterness and resentment, nor do you need to take your anger out on the wrong people. Although you may rage, your therapy helps you erect boundaries around your rage. You learn who deserves your anger and find ways to express it without hurting anyone, including yourself or selves. Anger is, indeed, a powerful emotion that can be frightening at times. When plumbed, explored, and safely expressed, it can also channel you into deeper healing.

*"In fact, negative emotions can be a positive step that leads toward healing."*

Slattery, mentioned earlier in this chapter, notes that anger may be important in setting boundaries, and doing so may create a positive sense of meaning where the survivor concludes, "My perceptions, needs, and feelings matter." She goes on, citing a research study: "In fact, for survivors of child abuse, forgiving oneself seems more related to decreased symptoms of PTSD than is forgiving the perpetrator."[24]

Remember, you're not a child anymore, you're an adult who's chosen a competent, trauma-informed therapist who will help nurture you and your parts through your emotions into healing. While negative emotions may feel uncomfortable, they're carrying the past that made you who you are today. You can come to value your negative feelings when you remind yourself that you're not there in the past, you're here in the present. You're a child who survived and grew into an adult who is giving your hidden child(ren) the chance to be heard.

Mike is my alter who carries my anger. From diffuse rage at everyone and everything, he gradually focused his anger on moving me forward and helping me confront myself about my unhealthy patterns. His passion pulled the rest of me out of despair when I most needed his help. In my memoir, I said:

> Over time, Mike's anger was the source of deep healing for me. His relentless drive to make our whole system healthy endowed him with the leadership my fragmented system needed. . . . Through Mike, I befriended anger and learned how to use it to my advantage without hurting anyone else. I lost my fear of anger and embraced the good it could do when channeled appropriately.[25]

Recovery from chronic early-childhood trauma is far more complicated than two choices: forgiving or not forgiving. When you enter into the healing process, let it take you where it leads. Toward the end of your journey, you may find yourself in a place of forgiveness. Or you may find yourself anywhere along a vast continuum of acceptance without forgiveness where healthy, happy, thriving people live.

## EXERCISE 10: CELEBRATING YOUR EMOTIONS

When your emotions are dissociated or compartmentalized into specific parts, it may be hard to get authentically in touch with them. It's common to experience numbness with no feelings at all, or emotions that burst forth like a volcano out of nowhere. Discovering, identifying, and expressing all of our emotions is an important part of our healing. Use this exercise to get in touch with your feelings.

On the left side of this page, make a list of all your negative emotions, like anger, rage, depression, worthlessness, and so on. Decorate them with crayons, markers, or stickers. They are your emotions, so celebrate them.

On the right side of this page, make a list of positive emotions, like happiness, optimism, peace, love, and so on. Add a few positive emotions you don't have now but want to grow in the future. These are yours too, so decorate and celebrate them.

## A FRESH START

As you travel the road to healing, you'll bump up against many obstacles, including potential expectations that you'll "forgive and forget" your perpetrator so that you—and everyone else—can get on with your lives. Now, though, you understand that jumping into forgiving at this point in your journey may not be in your best interest. There are other roads for you to travel. Forgiving is a possible outcome but not an inevitable one. You can leave this false start behind and start over. The hero is called to a fresh beginning that is focused on their needs, wants, and healing!

But first, let's look at several situations in chapters 3 and 4 that may need your forgiveness: forgiving yourself and forgiving friends and family who are otherwise trustworthy.

### SHARON'S STORY

Sharon is a middle-aged, happily married woman with two successful adult children. She graduated from college with a bachelor's degree in psychology and literature but decided, with her husband, to become a stay-at-home mom.

"Parenting my children is the best 'job' I ever had," she says, but then confesses, "To tell you the truth, my mental illness, in its different forms, prevented me from juggling family and career. I really could only do one."

In Sharon's early twenties, she had a tidal wave of flashbacks and memories that made her nonfunctional and resulted in her hospitalization. Over the next eight years, she was diagnosed, inaccurately, at different times by different therapists with a personality disorder, schizophrenia, and bipolar disorder.

"My favorite diagnosis," she says, "was 'difficult to treat.'" Sharon lost track of the medications she was given and the hospitalizations she experienced, many of which were retraumatizing.

One day in therapy, with yet another new therapist, she got up to leave the session, depressed and confused, with no memory of what had transpired. The therapist smiled and told her to have a great weekend. Something in that comment ignited Sharon, and her body came to life. With one foot already out the door, she felt herself hijacked, and a part she hadn't known existed took a backward step into the office, turned around, looked the therapist in the eye, and with a sassy new voice, firmly responded, "Oh, you bet I will!" Propelled forward by a new energetic force, the body strode cockily out of the building.

Thankfully, the therapist was astute and caught the drastic shift. Beginning the next week, they began exploring the accurate diagnosis that had been missed all those years—dissociative identity disorder. "Right away," Sharon says, "I knew she was right. The diagnosis, though scary to me at the time, was right."

Sharon severed ties with her parents once she had children. She remembers her father whispering a disgusting comment in her ear about what he'd do with her three-month-old daughter. "Something just clicked. I had not been safe growing up, but damned if I wouldn't do everything in my power to protect my children and, as it turns out, my own mental well-being."

Sharon equivocates on the word *forgiveness*. She was raised in the Roman Catholic Church, where she was taught the Ten Commandments and "to honor thy father and thy mother." Since both of her parents abused her, she has struggled with this commandment for many years. She no longer feels badly that she cannot honor the people who abused her.

"I do not hate them, nor do I love them, and I think that's okay. I understand that they brought forth their own hurts and traumas, and that, unfortunately, they just paid those forward to their offspring."

Sometimes Sharon refers to forgiveness as a long and complicated process that she's tackled as best she can. Sometimes she thinks acceptance might be a better word for the place of peace she has come to in her life. While she feels some compassion, she also believes they made choices, and she holds them accountable for those choices. Sharon believes that forgiving herself was more impactful than forgiving her parents.

"Dissociative identity disorder got me through the first eighteen years of my life. However, it's not been very helpful the past forty years. DID is just hard."

3

# THE INITIATION

*Forgiving yourself is the ultimate initiation.*

My son-in-law's grin lit up FaceTime. He laughed at my silly attempts at jokes, and he drew out his two children—my grandchildren—to tell me and my husband what was going on in their lives. Jeanie was in a school play and Will was interning with a local artist. We were fifteen hundred miles apart on two sides of the country, but these monthly gatherings kept us close. I reversed my camera and took them on a tour of our new Southwestern home.

"Here's our living room. Look at our cool wood viga ceilings. Here's our courtyard. We're going to put our hot tub here." We poked the lens outside and showed them our yucca and cacti.

"Cool," they said in unison. Our new desert life was alien to their lush East Coast greenery. After about half an hour, we said our goodbyes.

"Sending hugs! We miss you. Tell your mom I love her." They exchanged furtive glances with each other but put their smiles back in place as they waved goodbye.

My daughter was missing from this happy family conversation. By her choice. The publication of my memoir, the story of my discovery of and recovery from dissociative identity disorder, was too much for her to bear. Initially supportive of my journey, her tune changed when she saw our family story in black and white. At her request, I had changed her name, the names of her siblings, and the number and genders of siblings, and I removed at least one problematic story, but it wasn't enough. She pulled back in order to take care of herself.

I love my children. The early years of our lives were idyllic, and I reveled in mothering them. I hadn't planned on having children but, when they arrived, a new life-giving, joyful instinct emerged inside of me. We loved each other. No act of parenting these adorable little goofballs was too hard. All I wanted in life was to see them grow up happy and healthy.

How tragically ironic that what I wanted most was what I couldn't have. As I was decompensating many years ago, my elementary-aged daughter was huddled in a corner while her older brother slammed doors and screamed teenage obscenities and her younger brother banged holes in the wall of his bedroom. I knew our life was overwhelming her, as it was me, but I was impotent to help in any meaningful way. Without question, I abandoned my children emotionally so I could save myself. Each of my children chose a different way to cope. One used drugs, one moved away as fast as he could, and one got very, very angry. My daughter, I learned much later, dissociated, and the story of my memoir retraumatized her. How do I forgive myself for hurting the people I love most?

## LOVING YOURSELF

Forgiving yourself is a simple phrase that refers to the elusive task of loving yourself. As an infant, toddler, or adolescent, you may have internalized the message that you were unlovable and, in many cases, "to blame" for your family dysfunction in general and your own abuse in particular. You may have grown up believing you were defective and responsible for your parents' mistakes, your siblings' mistakes, as well as your own mistakes. Often, your love was contingent on meeting adult needs. Probably you developed a worldview that assumed you were unworthy of love. You might as well have a sign on your back that says, "Throw your disgust on me—I can take it!" Only you can't take it. Carrying other peoples' projections is hard for anyone, let alone a child, let alone many inner children.

*"Forgiving yourself is a simple phrase that refers to the elusive task of loving yourself."*

To make matters worse, the landscape of your abuse might have put you into an extremely compromising position where you were forced to hurt others, destroy property, or maim animals.[26] If that describes you, then you were brainwashed to believe this torture was your fault and your responsibility. Because you relied on your caregivers to give you warmth, love, and protection as all children do, you believed them—at least, parts of you believed them—when they forced their pathology on you. Like the rest of us, you probably fragmented to hold the contradictory images of your parents or caregiver because it was the only way you were able to survive.

You may have parts who hold unworthiness, parts who hold shame, as well as parts who hold confidence and competence. Rather than balancing each other out, these opposing self-images often lead to severe cognitive disorientation and internal conflict. For instance, as a whiz teaching children in the classroom but a failure parenting my own brood, I was prone to profound identity confusion. As you grow into adulthood, you may carry this confusion with you like a virus that affects the decisions you make, the relationships you engage in, and your understanding of self. You may hate yourself for being an innocent child who believed the lies. You may despise yourself for being a powerless young person who hurt others at the behest of a caregiver. You may loathe yourself for being an adult child who made mistakes while doing the best you could. Not only do you need to forgive yourself for believing the lie, you need to forgive yourself for others' sins perpetrated on you, and for your sins perpetrated on others. This is a new day, and you can make amends, where possible, and change your course to become the person you want to be.

Pete Walker, author of *The Tao of Fully Feeling*, says that blaming the source of abuse is an important step in loving ourselves. If we don't place blame on the authentic source, then we absorb it back into ourselves as shame. It is, he says, "a fundamental part of saying no, setting limits, protesting unfairness, and defending our boundaries. We will never feel safe if we cannot make blaming statements like: 'Stop it, you're hurting me!' 'Don't call me names!' and 'No, you cannot take that—it belongs to me!' Such reflexive blame is a vital contribution from the feeling nature to the instinct of self-protection."[27]

Our friend, Gabby, mulls over blame and self-forgiveness:

> *I continue to think, most of the time, that what happened to me as a child was my fault. I eventually need to let that faulty notion go if I'm to truly heal. I'm not sure that requires that I forgive myself, though. I think it requires an understanding of why I had to think that way to maintain the illusion of connection with the caregiver who was also my perpetrator, and why that perception is wrong. As someone with DID, though, I think there are persecutor parts who need to forgive child parts for simply being children and doing the best they could.*

Ultimately, learning how to love all of yourself—the good, the bad, and the ugly—is the foundation for forgiving yourself. Sometimes you may not like some of your parts' behaviors that may sabotage your good work, resist communication, or express powerful negative emotions that make you uncomfortable. It helps to remember that good parents of real children don't always like their behaviors either. But we love our children—both inner and real—in spite of their misbehavior, we set boundaries for them, and we shower them with patience.

As I began to meet my various insiders, my therapist always greeted them with, "Welcome. I'm so glad to meet you. I hope you'll come back again soon," even when the alters involved were angry and disruptive. She provided me with powerful role modeling—if she could love them, maybe I could too.

As my parts and I began to communicate, I often sent them love letters. *I don't know who you are, but I love you.* In the early days of my recovery, I wrote in my journal many times over, *Help me, help me, help me,* unaware of who was writing, whom I was writing to, or what the writing was about. As I began to learn my story, I frequently heard a voice whisper in my ear, "I love you, I love you, I love you." I didn't think it much mattered who was whispering or why. What mattered was someone inside loved me.

Walker says that we have two tasks when loving our inner children: "the recovery and ongoing development of our inborn sense of self-acceptance, and the reestablishment and strengthening of our instinctive sense of self-protection."[28] He calls these tasks "self-mothering" and "self-fathering," which, he notes, are inherently sexist phrases. Nonetheless, he believes that unconditional love and relentless self-protection help to clarify the distinctions between the two key processes of emotional support. When our inner children feel fully loved and fully protected, they are ready to forgive us, and we are ready to forgive them.

Kim is a trauma therapist with a DID diagnosis. When contemplating forgiving herself, she says:

> *Healing for me will require forgiveness and compassion, not for my perpetrators and abusers, but for myself, to conquer the shame, the rage, and the hate toward myself, toward the world, toward life, and the process it takes to become healed, healthy, real, alive, whole . . . to be present and engaged in living, maybe even thriving.*

Forgiving yourself is a critical part of your healing process. The foundation for forgiving yourself is loving yourself. Janina Fisher, clinician, researcher, and author of *Transforming the Living Legacy of Trauma*, says that "healing is the moment when we accept and forgive ourselves—the moment when we see that small child who we once were through the eyes of the compassionate adult we have become."[29]

## EXERCISE 11: WRITING A LOVE LETTER

**Write a love letter to yourself or to a part of yourself. Let yourself feel the love both as giver and receiver.**

### THE UNICORN SYSTEM'S STORY

Dr. Jamie Marich, author, therapist, and EMDR trainer, identifies as a bisexual, progressive Christian who was diagnosed with DDNOS (dissociative disorder not otherwise specified), a diagnosis now known as OSDD (otherwise specified dissociative disorder).

Jamie was raised by an evangelical fundamentalist father and a Roman Catholic mother who were, themselves, in conflict with each other's religious beliefs and transferred that conflict onto their children. Her memoir, *You Lied to Me About God*,[30] recounts this story.

The spiritual abuse Jamie experienced, along with childhood bullying and covert sexual abuse, resulted in dissociative coping strategies that became obvious in her early adulthood. Jamie struggled with drug and alcohol addiction—which is a self-medicating form of dissociation—in her early twenties, then learned from colleagues that her sober self was "zoning out, here but not here, present in body but not in mind." Once she was in addiction recovery, her inherent dissociation came into full bloom. Jamie was diagnosed at the age of twenty-five, and the Unicorn System was officially identified.

Jamie describes her healing as a series of layers beginning with her twelve-step recovery. Her sponsor was the first person to use the word trauma as, perhaps, relevant to her addiction. She was in a graduate counseling program at the time and launched into her own therapy to address the issues that were surfacing. EMDR (eye movement desensitization and reprocessing) was a game changer for Jamie and the foundation for the training program she subsequently developed for therapists at the Institute for Creative Mindfulness, which she founded. "Expressing myself through art and feeling my feelings without fear is a gift," Jamie says. Adhering to the adage "never once and done," her other layers of healing include shamanic practice, yoga, progressive Christianity, and more.

Jamie reflects on forgiveness, which she considers a religious term rather than a therapeutic term, and she believes she has forgiven her parents. "They would beg to differ though," she says. "As it relates to my father, we get along just enough to manage family events, but no more." She feels some compassion for them, but she doesn't excuse them. She accepts that they are who they are but wishes they would return the favor. "It sucks when the people who brought you into the world can't accept who you are," she says. "Or to know they believe you're going to hell." To augment the limited nature of her family relationships, she has built a large chosen family who has provided her with the support and unconditional love that each of us deserves.

From a professional perspective, Jamie doesn't believe forgiving is required to heal and she's not a fan of what she calls "lip service" forgiveness, which can get in the way of real healing. A fireball of energy, Jamie is devoted to advocating for normalizing dissociation and breaking down the stigma that surrounds it. To that end, she has written and published over fifteen books and manuals to help others heal and to help her fellow helpers.

When I asked Jamie if she believes there has to be participation on both sides of the forgiveness equation, she indicated she wasn't waiting around for her parents to hold court. If forgiveness helps her heal, she'll engage on her own. "I will not let the fuckers win," she concluded with a grin.

4

# COMPANIONS

*Trustworthy friends are priceless.*

I was waiting near the elevator used by airline personnel at the El Paso Airport. Arrivals were coming down the escalator, but my eyes were focused on the elevator where my dear friend of twenty years, Rhoda, would emerge. She was eighty-six years old, so we had arranged for a wheelchair to escort her through the airports from Missoula, Montana, to El Paso, Texas. I was just a few minutes late to pick her up for a ten-day visit in our new home in the Southwest desert.

*Could they have passed me on the way to baggage claim and I didn't see her?* Rhoda's visit would be an intimate reunion of old friends. I hadn't seen her for five years. She was a positive maternal figure for me as well as a spiritual guide. Shifting back and forth on my feet, I wondered if I should make a quick run back to baggage to see if I missed her. Before I could pivot, the elevator door opened and there she was.

A little befuddled at first, hunched over in her wheelchair, her eyes scanned the airport looking for something reassuring, then lit up when they met mine. She grinned widely and breathed a sigh of relief, and I grinned back as I walked toward her.

"I'm sooooo glad to see you," she said as she reached out to hold my hand.

"Me too," I whispered back as we hugged each other warmly, both happy that our time together was about to begin.

Fifteen years ago, this scene would never have happened. Rhoda was one of my first attempts at friendship post-therapy, and I was often triggered by her maternal persona that drew me toward her and repelled me at the same time. When she disappointed me—as was inevitable—she reminded me of my own mother who failed to protect me. After one particularly big disappointment, I was sure our friendship was over.

"How could you do this to me?" I cried as the weight of her decision sunk in. "You promised me!"

"I know, Lyn. I'm so sorry. I have to do what I have to do." Rhoda's apology was sincere, but it didn't calm my powerful feelings of anger, abandonment, and betrayal. She had lost my trust.

As luck would have it, we continued seeing each other by virtue of a shared community. I spent time with her when we were with other people, but I watched her very carefully and monitored my own reactions. When I felt overwhelmed with feelings, I took them to my therapist to process. I observed her kindness to me and to others, and I noticed others seemed to trust her too. My positive observations often balanced out my powerful negative emotions. Most of the time, I kept my distance, but sometimes I allowed myself to come closer.

"Lyn, you're such a good friend," she said as we carpooled to a community gathering one day. "You're so insightful," she continued. "You help me understand myself better than I already do." Year after year we stayed connected and slowly my defenses lowered. I began to see her not as my mother, but as a loving but imperfect person who was a faithful friend. Yes, she disappointed me, but no, she did not betray me.

"I love you, Rhoda," I told her one day. "And I forgive you for not being perfect," I added, tongue in cheek, knowing full well that none of us are perfect.

"I love you, too, Lyn. I'm not perfect, and I'm glad you accept me as I am." We both laughed and hugged over this moment of intimacy. Forgiving Rhoda wasn't intentionally a big deal. It was the slow process of unpacking my over-the-top feelings with my therapist and discovering, at the same time, that my friend was trustworthy. I often told her that she taught me how to forgive.

## CREATING HEALTHY RELATIONSHIPS

Friends you can trust are golden. They're the support that holds you upright in difficult times, the compassionate ear that actually listens, and the ones who go out of their way to be there for you. Even if you are an introvert, or someone who processes best alone, you are a social being. When you've been hurt by others, you still yearn for connection. Sometimes it feels like there's not a person in the world you can trust, yet you need good people in your life.

Maybe you've got this under control—you're surrounded by friends who have passed the test of time, you have a therapist who understands you, and maybe you even have a partner who will walk with you on your journey, or at least sit on the sidelines and wait for your return.

Or, you may struggle with relationships. Either you isolate yourself or you engage in friendships that are not healthy. You may erect walls to keep out people who are perfectly safe or refuse to set boundaries for people who walk all over you. Granted, there are periods in your life when you may not be the best of friends yourself, but as you heal, you can make choices that attract good people. Intentionally working on building healthy relationships is a worthy goal in therapy.

The best friends are trustworthy, even though they're imperfect. They're honest, compassionate, reliable, and have boundaries of their own. In other words, they're willing to "give" up to a point, but they won't go further than that point in order to take care of themselves. Rhoda set a boundary when she told me "I have to do what I have to do," even though her decision disappointed me.

You can learn from healthy friends how to be a friend yourself, including boundary setting. A boundary is a fence—not a wall—that you build for yourself to keep yourself healthy. You'll accept this behavior, but not that behavior. You'll give this much, but no more. You'll stay engaged unless this, that, or the other thing happens, and then you will disengage. You can't control another person's behavior, but you can control your own. Good friends will honor your boundaries. If you are being a good friend, you will honor their boundaries too.

Some people are truly not worthy of being your friend. They may be cruel, manipulative, or deceitful. They may have filled a need at one time in your life, but now that you're healing, you're looking for friends who are honest, compassionate, reliable, and have boundaries. Part of your healing process is to get better at recognizing the people who are safe and the people who are toxic, and to learn how to take appropriate action. The listening ear and wise guidance of a compassionate therapist will help to give you an honest reality check when you're dealing with friends, triggers, boundaries, and hard decisions about ending friendships.

Of course, as with all relationship issues you encounter, your fragmentation complicates the matter. In any circumstance, you may have parts who are ready to forgive at the drop of a hat and parts who want to banish a friend forever. My alter, the Black Knight, rode on his steed, swooped into my life, and vanquished the person in question whenever needed. This was the Black Knight's only role—to protect me from dangerous relationships—and he was usually unseen and unheard at other times. Sadly, he didn't have the whole picture in mind, or the context laid out on a spreadsheet, and it took time in therapy for him to give up the task of keeping us safe in such a dramatic manner.

> *"The best friends are trustworthy, even though they're imperfect."*

## FORGIVING FRIENDS AND FAMILY

Forgiveness, at its most basic level, is a coping skill. Everyone needs to develop this skill to navigate the common transgressions of life. When a friend neglects to answer your message, your feelings may be hurt. You may be triggered and respond the way you might have when you were truly abandoned. Instead of talking with them about what's going on, coming to some resolution, or even just letting it roll off your back, you may jump ship, back off, or walk away from the friendship. You may have an outburst and hurt your friend even more than they hurt you.

Everyone is human and makes mistakes, so a part of your healing work involves accepting these imperfections in yourself and others. Coming to a realistic understanding of who in your life is trustworthy and who does not deserve your trust will pave the way for you to forgive friends who prove themselves over time.

After many years of treatment, Judie, whom we met in chapter 2, still struggles with discerning whom she can trust:

> *I'm not totally confident in this since I had so many years of being "tricked" by my father and others. But I "hope" in the trust that I do give to certain people. And some, like my brothers for instance, I basically understand how much I can trust them. I have a hard time creating boundaries because I have never been given the right to do that. But I do keep trying and growing in that area. And where I have done so, it has essentially been good. Those who I put hope in trusting, I find that I can also forgive. If I can trust them, there is usually a certain amount of respect and even love, and I want to forgive them if it becomes necessary. I want people I can finally truly trust. I don't want to lose them or run from them. I want to learn where it is right to trust and forgive.*

Forgiveness, in the case of friendships, is a part of healing relationships, a part of becoming confident that you can recognize the nature of your friend's character, and a part of your growing maturity. You learn how to sit in the uncomfortable space of not knowing, observing, and then knowing after taking time to gather evidence. To heal from your trauma, you need to work through your triggers and use your creative mind to discern who is worthy of your forgiveness and who is not.

## EXERCISE 12: TRUSTING A FRIEND

**Think of a time when a friend hurt your feelings. Did this incident trigger you? Were you able to talk about the hurt? Overall, do you think this friend is trustworthy? If the answer is yes, can you forgive them, and if so, how will you go about conveying your forgiveness? If the answer is no, what will you do about it?**

## SHARRI'S STORY

Sharri is a wife, mother, nana, and overcomer of ritual abuse and mind control. As a young adult, she was aware of an experience where her father severely beat her with an aluminum flashlight when she was thirteen years old, but she had no emotion attached to the memory. Starting when her father died and gradually throughout her adulthood, she began to have flashbacks, fragments, and powerful emotions that were held by her identities and led to awareness of far worse torture, control, and trafficking.

Forgiving her perpetrators has been a part of Sharri's healing intention all along, but not without conditions. Sharri's healing from her complex history and her ability to forgive her perpetrators was made possible by the combination of her drive to heal, her loving husband, her Christian faith, and good therapy. But her work negotiating forgiveness with her identities is still ongoing. She outlines the process she takes in her forgiveness journey in this way:

Admitting that I was abused.

Accepting what was done to me by people who should have loved and protected me as well as greedy and power-hungry adults who exploited children through sex trafficking.

Putting the blame somewhere other than toward myself, which included accepting and loving myself and stopping the self-hatred.

Identifying and expressing the intense emotions of rage, anger, and hatred to release resentment, bitterness, and unforgiveness. Recognizing that holding onto unforgiveness was like drinking poison and expecting my abusers to die.

Seeing my abusers as people created in the image of God, who had been harmed as children and used as tools in the same evil that touched me.

Claiming my innocence as a child and reclaiming my present innocence as a child of God saved through Jesus Christ.

Knowing the true source of evil and admitting that Satan is the deceiver and father of lies who is out to steal, kill, and destroy (both my abusers and me).

Knowing Jesus as my savior, healer, protector, and friend who has overcome the world, sin, Satan, and death.

Knowing the hope there is because of Jesus and what He has done, the hope and assurance and security I have for eternal life with God my Father.

Knowing who I am in Christ and the identity I have because of Him as His beloved daughter.

Sharri says that automatically forgiving her perpetrators would have simply tapped into the mind control she had experienced as a child. She believes it was necessary to figure out who she was before she could truly forgive. Sharri believes that being able to give some of her history over to God has been helpful. She continues to do the work of healing, but, for some of her trauma, "it's for Him to sort out."

# 5

# THE THRESHOLD

*Once you've crossed the threshold, you can't go back.*

Over thirty years ago, I walked into Sonia's office for the first time, numb from the divorce from hell, terrified by what was happening to me and the family I thought I loved, leveled by a failed suicide attempt, and hopeful from a thirty-day hospitalization at a women's psychiatric unit. I thought I was a normal person with a normal life—college educated, married, with four wonderful children—but clearly I wasn't. Normal people don't have breakdowns.

Sonia's demeanor was warm and welcoming. Her smile was gentle, and her eyes reflected compassion even before she knew my story.

"Hello, Lyn. I'm glad to see you. Come in and sit down," she said.

I was fearful but I felt in my bones that taking this risk was my only choice. I had a new job as a teacher and had moved to a new community, trying to make a new start. I was in constant bodily and psychic pain with barely the energy to get up in the morning, let alone tackle a classroom full of twenty-five children.

"What would you like to talk about today?"

I thought I knew who I was, but there were parts of me making themselves known in the corners and recesses of my mind, leaving me feeling confused and chaotic. This new therapist welcomed even the most difficult parts of me.

"Everything everybody feels is okay, valid, and important," she said, turning my assumptions upside down. Her unqualified compassion awakened within me a buried seed of something close to trust. Taking a cautious step toward her was both painful and the unfamiliar fulfillment of a yearning.

The antidepressants prescribed by previous providers had been no help at all, so we ditched them from the get-go. With this new relationship that provided a growing sense of safety, my diagnosis moved with light speed from depression to PTSD to DID. On some days, it made no sense, and I couldn't imagine how this could be. On other days, it made perfect sense and resonated in the caverns of my consciousness. Maybe there was a reason for my disorientation and disjointed sense of self. Maybe I wasn't crazy after all.

"What's happening inside?"

My weekly ninety-minute sessions were an oasis in a desert of work, fractured family, and fractured self. That's not to say therapy was easy. It was excruciating. It was frightening. It was hard, hard work. But unlike my inner world elsewhere, I was real in those ninety-minute segments, as if a magnifying glass enlarged the truth of who I was twenty-four seven into that small, compressed period of time.

"Tell me about your family, Lyn."

With no memories, I was a walking testament to the aftermath of chronic early-childhood trauma. I had no idea what was ahead of me or how to get there. Forgiving was the last thing on my mind—first, because I didn't know whom to forgive or even what to forgive them for, and second, because all my energy was channeled into surviving and making it through each day. My goal, instead, was staying alive and maybe, just maybe, getting better. I put one foot in front of the other with no idea what recovery looked like.

I hoped Sonia would lead the way.

## TRUSTING SOMEONE

When small children, who have no resources of their own, rely on their parents, caregiver, or other adults for food, clothing, shelter, and love, and these same people abuse them, they're put in a confusing and volatile situation. *Should I stay close to this person I need for all aspects of my survival?* the child asks unconsciously. *Should I run away from the person who hurts me? What should I do if the person I need and the person who hurts me are the same?* Come close, run away, come close, run away. Love, hate, trust, fear, love, hate, trust, fear.

What a tragic predicament. Many small children develop attachment disorders from these contradictions. They spin back and forth between options leading nowhere, like a mouse running endlessly on a wheel. Like us, some fragment their minds into dissociative parts in order to survive what might otherwise be unsurvivable. As children, these parts are creative ways to endure a chaotic world where no one eases the pain or helps them process the trauma. As adults, they allow survivors to function in the real world while memory is tucked away in parts created for that purpose. These small children may grow into adults who have difficulty with intimate relationships. Functioning in the adult world, with the hidden history of an abused child revealed as fragments, can upend the brightest, most creative person. The long tail of trauma follows the child into every aspect of their adult life.

Is it any wonder, then, that the first baby step in healing—to trust someone—is perhaps the hardest task for adult survivors of chronic childhood trauma? Someone who will listen, who will believe, who will tell the truth? Someone who won't run away, who won't manipulate, who is a constant presence when childhood was a constant terror?

If you're lucky, you've already found a therapist who fits that bill and provides you with a safe space and soft landing that enables you to slowly develop the skills that you missed growing up in a traumatic environment. If you're not so lucky, you may have found that trusting a therapist isn't easy and finding the right one takes a long time.

Jumping from therapist to therapist is not uncommon. Sometimes it's for good reason, because there are some who don't understand trauma and do more harm than good. On the other hand, attachment issues, complicated by fragmentation, may prompt you to run away when you get too close to a therapist who's ready to be there for you.

If you find yourself moving from one therapist to another, it's worth examining the underlying reason. Can you speak to them honestly about your trust issues? How do they respond? Are they willing to slow down as you learn to trust? Have other clients found them trustworthy? The answers to these questions can help you determine if you need to walk out the door, or if it's worth taking the time to cultivate this new thing called intimacy.

> *"Is it any wonder, then, that the first baby step in healing—to trust someone—is perhaps the hardest task for adult survivors of chronic childhood trauma?"*

I began to know something was wrong when my family—a husband and four children under ten—began to split apart at the seams. What I didn't understand at the time was that I had alters taking charge with different capacities to parent and partner. My entry into therapy was driven by my failure in relationships but quickly grew into a whole myriad of issues such as suicidal ideation, body memory, and identity confusion. It took me quite a while to find the right therapist, but when I did, I grew by leaps and bounds. I dedicated my memoir to my therapist, who, I said, "helped me give birth to myself."

Learning how to trust a reliable therapist is critical. Trusting friends and support communities who allow you to be yourself and connect with others around shared experiences is also important. The writing group I founded that I mentioned in the beginning of this workbook grew into Dissociative Writers. I thought I was building a platform for my memoir. What I didn't expect was the organic way this group grew and diversified. When women and men came together to share their writing in a structured yet friendly group, they learned to trust themselves and each other. In a safe environment, people shared their vulnerabilities and bonded around common experience.

Today, this group has expanded to include people from all backgrounds with all levels of writing abilities from all over the world. Most importantly, we share our stories with other people who believe us. As we do this together, we are creating new pathways in our brain that help heal the damage we experienced. I discovered that my memoir, while important, was not the main event. The main event was and is the gathering of writers who trust each other!

Finding a therapist and other people you can trust is an important step in the healing journey.

## EXERCISE 13: FINDING YOUR HEALING GUIDE

**Do you have a good trauma-informed therapist whom you can trust? If you don't, Multiplied by One, *Psychology Today*, and the International Society for the Study of Trauma and Dissociation provide directories that you might want to explore.[31]**

**List the qualities you think are important for a therapeutic partner on your journey below. Or, draw a picture of you and your therapist working together to uncover and heal your wounds.**

## ESTABLISHING AN ENVIRONMENT FOR HEALING

In 1992, Judith Herman published the landmark book, *Trauma and Recovery: The Aftermath of Violence—From Domestic Abuse to Political Terror,*[32] which has informed trauma work worldwide since publication. In it, she lays out the three stages of recovery that she has witnessed in people who have experienced profound trauma. With great detail, Herman documents (1) the need for safety and stability before serious work on trauma can begin, (2) the memory work survivors engage in when they face the past, and (3) the reconstruction of a new life that's grounded in the knowledge the survivor has gained over the course of recovery. Herman calls these stages Safety, Remembrance and Mourning, and Reconnection.

As you begin to heal, Herman's stages set the perfect environment for your hero's journey. Among her many contributions, Herman's focus on safety and stability deserves further attention. It's important that your inner and outer worlds are safe and stable while engaging in trauma work. Literal safety from abusive people, with food, shelter, and supportive caregivers will allow you to lower defenses, recuperate, and get ready for the work of healing that's to come. Emotional safety can be just as important as you begin to surround yourself with people who listen, believe, and learn. It's very difficult to do serious recovery work when your physical and emotional safety are at risk. It certainly isn't healthy to consider forgiving a perpetrator at this stage of healing. All your energy is directed toward taking care of yourself.

Gabby, whom we met in chapter 1 of this book, reflects on safety and stability and suggests that moving through Herman's stages is cyclical rather than linear:

> *Stage one—safety and stability—comes up over and over for me, although less so the more therapy work I do. I'd say the bulk of the work I'm currently doing would fall into stage two—processing memories. At the same time, some stage three—integration and moving forward—is also happening.*

Judie, whom we met in chapter 2, agrees that it's unlikely these stages are linear. "It's more common there will be frequent returning to stabilization as the work enters new territory," she says.

We might think of the safety stage as similar to "home base" in a children's tag game: You can run all over the place but when the child who's "it" is getting close, you run back to home base where you're safe.

*"It's important that your inner and outer worlds are safe and stable while engaging trauma work."*

When Janice, a lawyer and a mother, checked herself into a psychiatric hospital, she had survived one suicide attempt, the emotional abuse of her husband from whom she was then separated, and the chaotic, sometimes violent outbursts from her confused and frightened children. She had been diagnosed with depression, but her antidepressants were ineffective. She functioned well in her professional life but was unable to carry that competence into her personal life. A myriad of internal voices common to dissociative disorders, and not to be confused with the external voices of schizophrenia, were draining her will to live.

Entering a well-designed psychiatric program for thirty days helped her inner world stabilize. When she was discharged, she followed through on plans made with the help of the hospital staff to move to a different city and begin a new job. Her husband agreed to take one child, and she took the other, further stabilizing her. The anger and violence in the family was reduced, and she found a new trauma-informed therapist, all of which increased her sense of safety. This safety and stabilization enabled her to begin deep work, which uncovered chronic childhood trauma in her history. Prior to stabilization, it had been unsafe for her to begin that exploration. Her treatment progressed, and she was diagnosed with OSDD, or otherwise specified dissociative disorder.

Safety and stability are not unrealistic goals to reach but a general state of assurance that your physical needs will be met and your emotional needs have an outlet with a trained trauma therapist. As Gabby and Judie noted, it's not uncommon to cycle back to this stage when old traumas or new stressors arise. Approach the reestablishment of safety and stability over the duration of your recovery as a matter of course. As you will see shortly, the Healing Wheel is demanding and will stretch your capacity more than once. Knowing you can slow down, seek help, and give your insiders a break can make all the difference.

## EXERCISE 14: EXPLORING SAFETY

**What does safety mean to you? Using words or art materials, create an image—real or imaginary—that conveys safety to you.**

## THE LAY OF THE LAND

Finding a therapist that you trust, achieving safety and stability, and doing the work of healing is the lay of the land for any trauma survivor. If your trauma occurred in childhood and you used dissociative coping strategies to protect you from its chronic impact, your terrain will be similar to Herman's stages, but your road map will have specific highways and byways that accommodate your dissociative experience. As you cross the threshold, you're creating an environment that will enable you to become the hero of your own journey. As you navigate the Healing Wheel found in the next chapter, you'll be embarking on your quest to actualize your healing intention.

Let's go!

### BONNIE'S STORY

In her young adulthood, Bonnie was a bright go-getter who broke glass ceilings working in state- and national-level government in health and human services. Her training as a linguist had taken her around the globe to work in other countries, but she eventually returned to the United States, where she became an advocate for children and families. Bonnie was living the dream with a fulfilling career, a loving husband, and two children when it all began to fall apart at the age of fifty. After several physical breakdowns over a period of six years, Bonnie landed in a wheelchair with no apparent cause.

Bonnie's primary care doctor could find nothing medically wrong with her, nor could a world-class neurologist find any neurological issues. When Bonnie shared that she had attempted suicide at the age of twelve, the neurologist said, "When you find the reason your twelve-year-old self wanted to die, you'll know the cause of your physical disabilities." That was the beginning of healing for Bonnie, who reluctantly engaged a psychologist as alters began to emerge. Today, after many years of inner work around incest, ritual abuse, mind control, and the wisdom she gleaned from indigenous spirituality, Bonnie is physically healthy and happy. You can read more about Bonnie's story in her memoir, *An Apparently Normal Person.*[33]

When I asked Bonnie if forgiving her perpetrators was a part of her healing journey, she answered without hesitation, "No!" Then she thought about it some more and said, "For me, compassion was more important than forgiving." Bonnie went on to talk about her exploration of indigenous spirituality, a path that took her to a large gathering of indigenous peoples in Peru, where people were praying for their ancestors in order to bring healing and peace. "Twelve generations of ancestors," she said. "They were asked to pray for twelve generations of their ancestors in order to release them from the pain they had endured."

Like a thunderclap, Bonnie realized that she should be praying for twelve generations of her ancestors too. Her experience with her indigenous friends was as much about her history as it was about their history. "I realized that my ancestors and I had been dancing an intergenerational dance. I had been successful in breaking the cycle of fear and violence, but my perpetrators were still stuck in that dance. They needed healing as much as I did, for the pain they had endured, for the pain they had inflicted, and for the soul wounds that were perpetuated across generations." Bonnie knew at some deep level that it didn't matter that she didn't know them or what had happened to them or the atrocities they had committed. "The only thing that mattered was that I was praying for them and releasing them. This was my job. It was the reason I had come into the world—to break the cycle."

Bonnie discovered that it was important for her to express her rage before being able to release her ancestors. In the quiet of the morning under a canopy of oak trees at a local public park, adult Bonnie allowed her insiders to create a personal ritual of healing. She stormed around the secluded space, swearing like a sailor, picking up little sticks from the ground. *These look like penises*, she thought, and began to name them one by one for the men whose penises had violated her, then branched out to include "every man who puts his penis where it doesn't belong and any man who tries to control someone else." Bonnie's wrath knew no bounds as she felt anger pouring out of every pore of her body. Guided from inside, she built a bonfire to consume the symbolic "penis sticks." Watching their destruction by fire and their remnants rise in smoke, she broke into tears and invited every alter to come forward, each sobbing deeply as new waves of smoke, representing each past generation, ascended into the atmosphere. "I saw their pain in the smoke," Bonnie said. "It sounds woo-woo, but it was palpable and real."

That's when Bonnie began to exercise her compassion muscle, to understand at a deeper level how wounded her perpetrators were to do the horrible things they did. "For me, forgiveness wasn't necessary. I never said the word, and some of my insiders were adamant there was no way that was going to happen. Compassion, on the other hand, was critical. I have compassion for my perpetrators and the pain they endured. I've released them."

# 6

# THE QUEST

*The work of healing is the point.*

"I don't like her. You're the only one I can talk to about this besides our group facilitator," I said to another woman who was in the group I was attending with other dissociative survivors. "She reminds me of my father. Or maybe my sister. But I don't trust her. I think she may hurt me." I was referring to Sara, a woman with a strong personality, not unlike me, who seemed to haunt me in our group setting. I was not only triggered by her, but I transferred onto her; she was alternately my father, my sister, even my submissive mother who never protected me.

Fortunately, my therapist was the person who ran the group, so I could take my terror and fear back to the therapy room. "Why didn't you protect me?" I'd demand from Sonia when she didn't step into a disagreement between Sara and me.

"Why would I protect you?" she'd say. "She didn't do anything to hurt you. Besides, you're an adult and perfectly capable of protecting yourself." The icing on the cake was when Sonia suggested I disliked Sara because she was so much like me. We were alike? *How dare she*, I thought. *Comparing me to Sara. I'm not like her. I'm . . . different.*

I was terrified to go to group. Everyone, not only Sara, seemed to pose a threat. I negotiated with my alters to determine who would attend and who would stay home. It never worked out the way I planned, and I often came home suicidal. When I explained my conundrum to another woman in the group, she looked at me incredulously and said, "Why do you go at all?"

I didn't have an answer for her. I just knew I had to venture into the lion's den every week—for years—to conquer the triggers, transform the fear, and prepare myself for the whole life I was seeking.

## THE HEALING WHEEL

The healing journey requires the hero to plunge into work that's daunting and difficult. Luckily, the drive to heal is greater than the drive to avoid the pain at all costs, so you're probably already knee-deep in the thickets of recovery. With your healing intention in your pocket to chart your destination, the Healing Wheel (see graphic 1) is the map that will help you get there.

Using the Healing Wheel as a graphic organizer, you can anticipate what your unique healing path might look like. From the top of the wheel, and moving clockwise, (1) you'll discover who you are by working with your parts, your memory, and identity, (2) you'll work on shame, trust, and relationship issues, (3) you'll learn how to manage your triggers and feel all your feelings, (4) you'll grieve the loss of your fantasy childhood, (5) you'll learn how trauma impacts survivors in general, and how it has impacted you specifically, (6) you'll explore ways to claim surrogate justice, and (7) you'll build a new future and eventually find peace.

Each spoke of the Healing Wheel represents a facet of the healing process outlined above, not in a linear or orderly fashion, but in a ubiquitous, spontaneous, and ongoing manner that's specific just to you. These different work areas are represented graphically as equivalent in size and revolving around the hub, which is a whole life.

In reality, you may spend more time on one work area than another, but in the end, you'll work on every one. In the case of coexisting conditions, you may have issues not represented in the Healing Wheel to add to the mix. You may be working on one, two, or even seven areas at a time, as each area impacts and relates to the other work areas.

It's helpful if you can space out your work so it's manageable; if you're like many of us, you'll go through some periods that feel like a marathon or a clown juggling too many balls. Like a rider on a cross-country bike trip, you'll pedal through all of these spokes and more.

Graphic 1

The Healing Wheel is not intended to replace the work of healing. Reading about the work of healing is not the same as *doing* the work of healing. Rather, the Healing Wheel will provide you with a map, so you know what's up ahead. In truth, this journey will take years, maybe even decades, to travel, so take your time, prepare well, and create soft landings for the hard times ahead.

It's helpful to note that the Healing Wheel aligns well with Judith Herman's stages of recovery we encountered in chapter 5. The specificity of the spokes of the Healing Wheel and, in some cases, the intensity of the work, surpasses that of Herman's stages due to the developmental impact of chronic trauma on children.

The vast expanse of your journey is the quest for a *whole life.*

Let's take a deep dive.

*"With your healing intention in your pocket to chart your destination, the Healing Wheel is the map that will help you get there."*

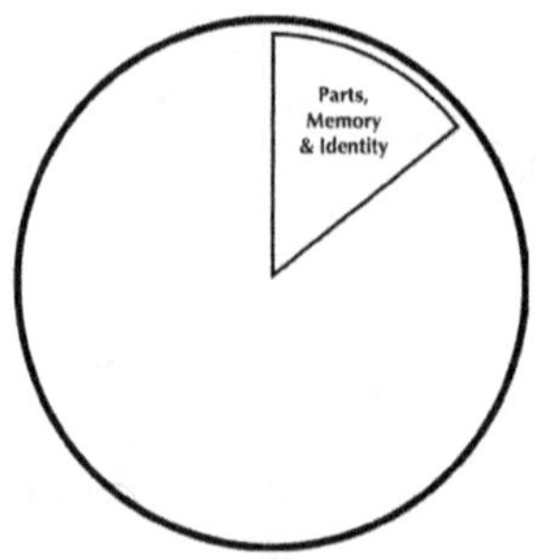


## PARTS, MEMORY, AND IDENTITY WORK

Remembering our trauma is often thought of as the "meat" of healing, but it's far more complicated than just remembering. The goal is to mine your body, mind, and spirit for the truth of your trauma, and to integrate it into the person you are becoming. In doing so, you will know your history from your authentic perspective and release the pain that's been holding you captive. By remembering your trauma, you are embracing the narrative that was denied to you by your abuse. You are reconstructing your past, present, and future with new knowledge.

Remembering your trauma doesn't always mean you'll have crystal clear memories. Research over the last thirty years has demonstrated that the brain works differently when confronted by a dangerous situation. Instead of sending images to the front or thinking brain, which holds everyday memories, it sends the message instantaneously into the body, where our ancestors had a chance to save themselves from the tiger by fighting, fleeing, or freezing. We call this the fight, flight, or freeze response. For a small child, freezing is often the most viable response when a caregiver twice their size is raping them in a dark room or beating them in broad daylight. Sometimes the child has the opportunity to fight or run away, but letting it happen and getting it over with is often the most effective survival response in the moment.

Further, we know trauma shuts down the thinking brain, which takes too long to respond. Instead, emotions and instinctive responses lodge in the back or emotional brain and in the body. Imagine you are crossing the street and see a car speeding toward you, only a few feet away from making impact that will almost certainly kill you. Your thinking brain shuts down so your body response can prompt you to flee as fast as you can and get out of the way of the oncoming car.

When the crisis is over and you're safe once again, you think back about what happened. You may not remember anything surrounding the near miss. People ask you about the car—what color was it? what make? what license plate?—but you have no idea, because your thinking brain was offline. In the days and weeks following, you feel periods of terror and anxiety, especially when you enter a busy thoroughfare, and your recall may be accompanied by elevated heart rate, dizziness, nausea, or hot flashes.

Years later, you may forget the incident entirely, but your back brain and body doesn't. Out of the blue (or so it seems), you begin to feel terror, anxiety, nauseousness, and dizziness whenever you walk down a busy street. These are traumatic memories. The street is a trigger that sends you back to your past. Your thinking brain has no idea why you are experiencing anxiety because it never received a full narrative of the crisis event. Now, over time, what little knowledge you had of your near miss has disappeared. You're left with emotions and body memories without a narrative. You can read more about trauma and the brain in appendix B.

If this is how the body and mind respond to a single traumatic adult experience, imagine the intensity of response when the trauma happens over and over again to a small child. The process of triggering is the same, but the power and impact of the memory is multiplied many times. Bessel van der Kolk, trauma researcher and author of *The Body Keeps the Score: Brain, Mind, and Body in Trauma Healing*, says, "The imprints of traumatic experiences are organized not as coherent logical narratives but in fragmented sensory and emotional traces: images, sounds, and physical sensations."[34] He points out that, often, there is little or no story to tell. All this is to say that your memories may be fragmented, located in your body rather than your mind, and lacking a cohesive narrative.

> *"Remembering your trauma doesn't always mean you'll have crystal clear memories."*

Janina Fisher, whom we met in chapter 3, says, "A traumatic event is not over when it is over—even if we have successfully survived."[35] Fisher notes that trauma is remembered more emotionally and somatically than in narrative form so "survivors often feel confused, overwhelmed, or crazy. Without a memory in words or pictures, they do not recognize what they are feeling as memory."[36] Fisher further explains that even our triggers are memories and encourages us to treat them as such. "I encourage you to assume that any highly distressing or overwhelming emotion that you do not understand might be a trauma symptom,"[37] Fisher says.

Unlike other trauma survivors, most people with dissociative coping strategies have parts that carry memories. Welcoming your parts, learning about their role in your system, and encouraging communication between and among them is an important part of your work. As your parts begin to tell their stories, the walls of amnesia surrounding them begin to lower, and knowledge begins to move fluidly between them so that you—the physical person—can navigate through life with more self-knowledge.

This is called *integration*: the combining of one thing with another so that they become whole. There's a good deal of disagreement among people with dissociative disorders over the issue of integration, which is also called *fusion* by the International Society for the Study of Trauma. While many people look forward to full integration as their goal, some prefer to remain in collaborative parts after addressing the other work areas of recovery, otherwise known as functional multiplicity. Whether your parts integrate into one whole person, or whether they remain in parts with full collaborative knowledge of one another, the sharing of knowledge between parts is still called integration. As we heal, we integrate.

Identity work grows from the relationships you build with your parts. When you started your healing process, you may have experienced identity confusion. I knew myself as Lyn, but who were these parts that were claiming names? The issue was existential: Who am I? The answer emerges out of the long, slow process of getting to know yourself, or your selves, through your alters, your traumatic memories, and your triggers, and through addressing the other areas of recovery work.

The word *switching* refers to the dissociative movement from one part of ourselves to another. Sometimes others may notice that movement before we do, and sometimes we notice that movement internally but do not reveal it to others. Do you have dramatic mood swings for no apparent reason, memory lapses, or the sense that you're not the person you thought you were? What about feeling disoriented or gravitating toward different mannerisms, clothing styles, or food preferences? These might be signs that you are switching between parts. On the other hand, some people don't experience obvious signs of switching and manifest their parts subtly and covertly, hiding the truth even from themselves.

In my memoir, I described dissociative switching as "icicles" swaying in the back of my brain, ready to protect me from whatever danger I perceived was before me. Olga Trujillo, author of *The Sum of My Parts: A Survivor's Story of Dissociative Identity Disorder*,[38] uses the image of cotton filling her head each time she was raped. Shelley Kolton, author of *Brain Storm: A Life in Pieces*,[39] says, "I always felt like something was crawling up my neck and hair before I dissociated." Regardless, switching between parts is a protective dissociative mechanism that, when explored, can lead you to a deeper understanding of who you are.

At times, you may be devastated to learn the truth, but you may also be exhilarated when you gain the power to shape yourself or selves into the future. Socrates and other ancient Greek philosophers admonished us to "know thyself," promoting the truth that self-knowledge is power. Those of us who recover from dissociative disorders know ourselves better than most other people ever will, and, from that new reality, we claim the power to be who we were meant to be. In the past, you were controlled. Today, you have control.

## EXERCISE 15: PARTS CAN CHANGE YOUR LIFE

**Draw a picture of the part(s) of you who has (have) the power to change your life. Let those parts write about how they want to navigate your present circumstances and your future hopes.**

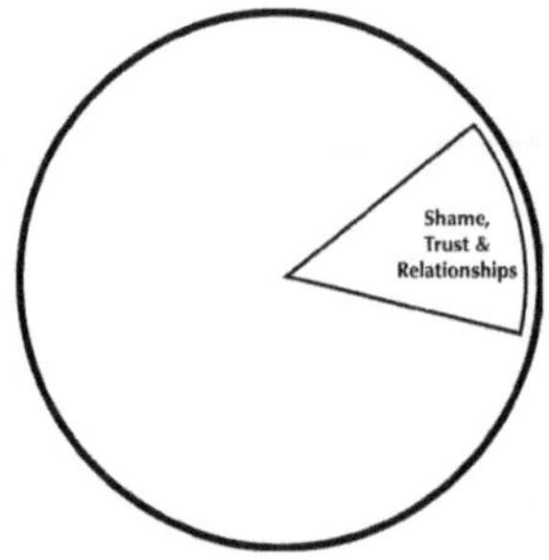


## SHAME, TRUST, AND RELATIONSHIPS

Speaker, writer, and researcher Brené Brown defines shame as intensely painful feelings or experiences of believing that we are flawed and therefore unworthy of love and belonging—that something we've experienced, done, or failed to do makes us unworthy of connection. "I don't believe shame is helpful or productive," she says. "In fact, I think shame is much more likely to be the source of destructive, hurtful behavior than the solution or cure."[40] Brown concludes that using shame as a disciplinary technique does more harm than good.

You may walk around with a ton of shame that doesn't belong to you. Your caregivers may have told you that you weren't good enough, or that you were responsible for bad things that weren't in your control, or that you were flawed and defective. For some survivors, the seeds of shame were implanted as a method of control. Growing up with those sometimes overt and sometimes subliminal messages were enough to convince you to shame yourself without the help of other people. If you were alone on a desert island, you would probably feel the shame just as you do in a crowded city or at your family of origin's dining room table. If you're like me, it follows you everywhere you go. It's not what we are, it's who we are, or at least that's how we feel. Our old tapes have convinced us that our very existence is shameful.

Destroying those old tapes and replacing them with the truth that you're a worthy human being who deserves a happy life takes time. Wrenching your self-esteem from the tentacles of shame is like cleaning an oven that never comes clean. Writing and repeating daily affirmations helps to build the truth of who you are and negate the lie that was told to you. Or, you can give your shame back to the people to whom it belongs—the ones who created the old tapes in the first place—by journaling, role play, or even actual confrontation (only with your therapist's help, please). Or, if your shame resides in an alter, you can help your insider release the shame by treating them with the love and respect you never received.

My shame was an organ in the middle of my chest that pumped black tar into my body much like the heart pumps blood into fingers and toes. Eventually, this organ told me his name—Devil—and revealed he was an infant. My whole system gathered around to comfort him when he cried and cried and cried. I believe that each tear sent a little bit of shame out of my body and into the atmosphere to be transformed into something good. Thirty years later, Devil changed his name to Angel. My shame still peeks out every now and then, but I understand it's a feeling and not a testament to who I am.

Shame can lead to distorted relationships. Its insidious message tells you that if you're "bad," then you deserve bad relationships. Equally damaging, it declares that you don't deserve anything better. Loving yourself and forgiving trustworthy friends and family members, the theses of chapters 3 and 4, can lead to healthy relationships and dismantle shame's power. Self-love and equitable partnerships send the countervailing message that you are worth something and you deserve good people in your life.

Trust, or the lack of it, also distorts relationships. Trusting someone who is trustworthy is the bedrock of your recovery, as we learned in chapter 5. Testing the waters with a therapist, a family member, or a friend is a huge risk. They might hurt you, they might betray you, they might abandon you. Yet taking the risk and learning from whatever unfolds is critical for your growth. Did you discover that this person is toxic and not a good candidate for a relationship? Is that person someone you can rely on and definitely friendship material? As an adult who now cares for your inner children, you can soothe those who are disappointed, give courage to those who are afraid, and applaud those who took the risk to trust. Looking at your relationships—both friendships and romantic interests—through the lens of the healthy person you want to become can empower you to make choices that are right for you.

*"Each small success in every area of recovery helps to enlarge your self-worth and reduce the impact of your toxic past."*

Expecting to overcome your obstacles to healthy relationships in one fell swoop is unrealistic. Your entire healing journey is the mechanism by which you will ultimately gain power over shame and misplaced trust. As with everything else, taming your inner demons and putting them in their place takes time. Each small success in every area of recovery helps to enlarge your self-worth and reduce the impact of your toxic past. From that place of power, you begin to trust yourself, trust the people who deserve your trust, and cultivate positive relationships that enhance your life. You no longer mindlessly follow the worst of humanity but rather make good choices to find the best that humanity has to offer. When you heal your shame and learn to trust, you'll find yourself engaging in relationships that are worthy of who you are, because you're worth it.

## EXERCISE 16: HEALTHY PRIDE

**Make, do, or create something that makes you proud. This could be playing with a child, taking your dog for a walk, creating a collage, playing the piano, giving a homeless person a dollar, or any of many possibilities. Write about the experience here. Let your pride replace your shame. How does that feel?**

## MANAGING TRIGGERS AND FEELING FEELINGS

Dissociation saved us by separating our trauma from parts of ourselves. Our bodies and our minds split, temporarily, so that we could manage in real life. Our minds went to one or more places while our bodies experienced the trauma. If trauma was chronic, our splits were less temporary and became the go-to way we coped with life, from childhood into adulthood. Today, we pay homage to this coping strategy of disconnection between thoughts, memories, and actions, while, at the same time, recognizing its negative impact on our lives as functioning adults.

As an adult, you may experience dissociation as a sense of unreality in relation to yourself or selves and to the world around you. You may watch yourself go through the motions of life from the outside looking in. You may lack memories from the day before or from a chunk of your childhood. You may, at times, feel like someone else entirely and discover, maybe to your chagrin, that, indeed, you do have different parts or personalities inside. All of this may add up to a pervasive sense of numbness. Each of us experiences dissociation uniquely, but these are some of the main descriptors of dissociation in adults.

Yet feelings in the dissociative person are often in short supply. It's not that they're not there, it's that they're hidden away in the pockets of our minds and bodies that were created by dissociation. Dissociation prevents us from feeling all our feelings in the way that people who haven't experienced trauma feel them. Instead, we may feel numb or overwhelmed by too many feelings all at one time.

Numbing is a protective mechanism that keeps us from feeling the feelings from the past, as well as feeling our feelings in the present. Shutting down our historical memories may have served a useful function at one time, but it also prevents us from living a full life in the here and now. We deserve to feel the full range of emotions in the present—love, joy, fear, competence, anger, contentment, pride, agitation, and more. These feelings are the mark of being human. When our emotional switch flips off, we lose an important part of ourselves.

Emotional flooding may seem the opposite of numbing, but they are related. Like the fiery molten rock inside a volcano that can no longer remain underground, our dissociated feelings burst out into the open with such a force that we are buried by their intensity. The ensuing chaos makes it difficult to identify separate feelings and we are at the mercy of the deluge. Although emotional flooding may be initiated by a variety of stimuli, triggers from the past is one of them.

Because the trigger, or trauma memory, is in the body rather than in the narrative brain, we usually have no idea of the root cause of our flooded feelings. Instead, we feel afraid, enraged, or doomed in the present day even though we know, at least at some level, that we are safe, competent, and able to take care of ourselves. An important part of healing is learning how to manage our triggers to make room for our real feelings that are connected to both the past and the present.

> *"We deserve to feel the full range of emotions in the present—love, joy, fear, competence, anger, contentment, pride, agitation, and more."*

Each of us learns what helps to ground us in the present when our minds and bodies are taking flight into the past. This may include physical activity like walking, dancing, yoga, or other bodily movement. Some people use the arts, like music, crafts, painting, drawing, and writing, to bring themselves back from the past into the present. Still others find that talking with their therapist is the only way to break the bubble of a trigger. For myself, I found that getting back out there and learning that I was capable in "this" world helped to pull me back from my helplessness of "that" world.

Janina Fisher emphasizes the need to work through our powerful feelings to determine where they come from and what they mean for us, today, in the present:

> In order to know where we are and who we have become despite the trauma, we have to learn how to discriminate between a here-and-now emotional reaction and a feeling or body memory. To know we or those around us are safe, we have to make those discriminations. Otherwise, we will automatically trust those who do not trigger us and distrust all those who do. We will believe the shame is a truth about ourselves rather than understand it as a memory. We will interpret fear as a sign that we are not safe.[41]

For years I was either flooded with feelings that had no context, or numb and without feeling, sometimes both at the same time. By the time I found my therapist and began seeing her on a regular basis, I was totally confused about feelings. I was sure my real feelings were bad and proof that I was a defective person. I thought, *It's bad to be angry. It's bad to be afraid. It's bad to be sad. I don't know how to be happy. I'm so confused.*

One day, my therapist told me, "Everything everybody feels is okay, valid, and important." I was overwhelmed by these profound words that touched the parts of me who were sure that I was defective. I went home and made a primitive poster to remind all of myself of my therapist's affirmation: *Everything everybody feels is okay, valid, and important.*

When we expel the poison of old tapes, toxic shame, and past abuse, we discover the freedom to experience both positive and negative feelings in real time. Our emotional space expands to embrace the whole range of human emotions in the present. Our inner landscape has room for new feelings, new thoughts, and new awarenesses that feed our bodies, minds, and spirits. Feeling our real feelings in the here and now is an experience no longer confused by dissociation, silenced by numbness, or overshadowed by triggers.

## EXERCISE 17: TAKE A FEELINGS WALK

**Take a "feelings" walk around your indoor living space, your yard, or your neighborhood. Look at your surroundings while you're walking. Tread lightly when you feel good, walk heavily when you feel bad. If you feel angry, allow yourself to stomp.**

**If you have mobility impairment, take a finger walk around an imaginary space in front of you. If you feel good, make your fingers create a happy place. If you feel angry, pound your fist (without hurting yourself) or use another hand motion to convey your anger.**

**Record your walk below.**

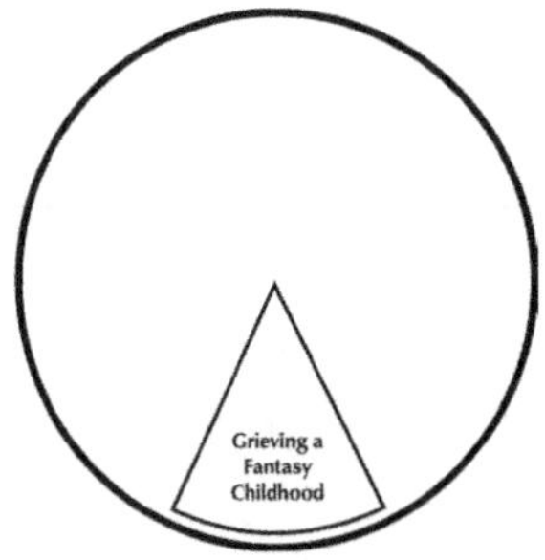


## GRIEVING A FANTASY CHILDHOOD

Coming to terms with the lack of a coherent narrative can trigger a grief process that's woven throughout your recovery. The childhood you thought you had may be replaced by memories you find hard to believe. The life you are living as an adult is tainted by forces outside your consciousness. The person you thought you were may not be the person you're experiencing now. Like many of us, you may find that your whole world has been turned upside down and you're shaken to your core. Grieving the loss of the world you thought you knew is an important part of your healing journey.

Over the course of my life, I have lost many things that were important to me. To name a few, I lost the family I created to divorce, a loving second husband to premature death, a safe home and community to a move, and a child to the legacy of my trauma. Perhaps the most profound loss was the childhood I never had.

In a sense, this primary loss seems a bit of a stretch since I have so few memories of childhood. When I compare my few happy recollections with the happy lives of children I know in the present, I was severely lacking. But you don't know what you don't know, and I didn't know my childhood wasn't happy. Not until I began to heal did I realize that my recollections of my early years were a fantasy of the childhood I never had. Facing the truth about my life was the biggest loss.

The original five stages of grief were observed and recorded in 1969 by Elisabeth Kübler-Ross, MD, in her book *On Death and Dying: What the Dying Have to Teach to Doctors, Nurses, Clergy, and their Own Families,*[42] which was based on her work with terminally ill patients. Those include denial, anger, bargaining, depression, and acceptance. Since then, other models with other stages have been developed to describe the slow process of coming to terms with loss. Some models add creating meaning out of loss, or finding purpose, or reconstruction, or some other way to describe the new you who emerges from the rubble.

While the stages of grief were originally articulated in terms of loss through death, there is general consensus that grief is a product of many kinds of losses: death, divorce, catastrophic illness, loss of job, loss of financial security, loss of a dream, loss of a sense of self. It should come as no surprise, then, that those of us who experienced chronic early-childhood trauma might grieve the loss of the childhood we never had.

"What!" you might say. "I not only have to work with my parts, contend with my memories, and deal with shame, trust, and relationship issues, but I also have to grieve the loss of my fantasy childhood, too? Dealing with triggers, identity confusion, and constant psychic pain isn't enough? It's not fair!"

You're right. It's not fair. If you walked away in a huff (for only a few minutes), I'd understand! But fair or not, grief is part of the hand we've been dealt.

Cathy Collyer, a Dissociative Writer member, licensed health care provider, and author of *Staying in the Room: Managing Medical and Dental Care When You Have DID*,[43] says she still grieves every day and believes that's the cost of experiencing chronic childhood trauma. "The triggers for my grief are in everyday life," she says. "It no longer immobilizes me. I accept that it's a part of healing from trauma, and that it will hit me coming out of left field as often as it can be anticipated. The more skilled I become at grieving loss, the healthier I become."

Wherever you are in your healing, think about the stages of grief and which ones you've experienced. Have you ever denied the memories your parts share with you, or did you deny your diagnosis? Denial is a common first response when the false image we've created begins to crumble. Anger is a hard one, and many of us have trouble getting in touch with our anger for fear it may do irreparable harm to ourselves or someone we love. Yet buried within our systems are red molten lava streams of rage seeking expression. What about bargaining? In my memoir, *Crazy*, I remember a conversation I had with my insiders just prior to diagnosis.

"I'm not a multiple personality, but I am screwed up and very confused. If I forget about names and just talk about feelings, then it will be okay."[44]

I suspect we've all experienced a deep sadness that may have been diagnosed as depression. For many of us, a diagnosis of depression may be what led us into therapy. When you think about it, depression is a rational response to coming face-to-face with our truth. Sometimes medication helps to take the edge off; other times, giving our alters a voice lifts the heaviness so we can continue to do our work.

Like the whole healing process, grief has its own timeline, and everyone experiences it differently. The stages aren't linear, nor are they orderly. Just as we move in and out of the seven spokes of the Healing Wheel, we also move in and out of the stages of grief. For some of us, it's a lifelong process of difficult discovery; for others, it's a celebration of release. Your method of grieving will be different from mine, and mine will be different from someone else's. We are unique human beings who've experienced unique trauma in unique times and places. Our "new normal" will be ours alone as we move toward acceptance.

Acceptance, of course, is the goal we all seek, to come to some sense that the past is in the past, but now we can change the trajectory of our lives because we are in the present and creating the future. Kübler-Ross's concept of acceptance as a stage of grieving is very similar to Janis Abrahms Spring's concept of acceptance as a form of forgiveness and the Finding Future, Purpose, & Peace spoke of the Healing Wheel. Understandably, in this stage of grief, some of us may entertain the possibility of forgiveness. For those with religious or other incentives, forgiveness may well be the next step. For many, however, forgiveness isn't necessary in order to complete the grieving process.

> *"Like the whole healing process, grief has its own timeline, and everyone experiences it differently."*

## EXERCISE 18: GRIEVING WITH MUSIC

**Sometimes music brings forth feelings that come with grief. Sometimes it soothes us, sometimes it empowers us, sometimes it brings us to tears. Music can help us through the grieving process.**

**Play some music that touches your soul. Is it rhythmic, upbeat music? Classical symphonic? Down-home folk? Sorrowful and soulful? Let the music bathe you in whatever feeling you may be feeling in the moment. Record this experience below.**

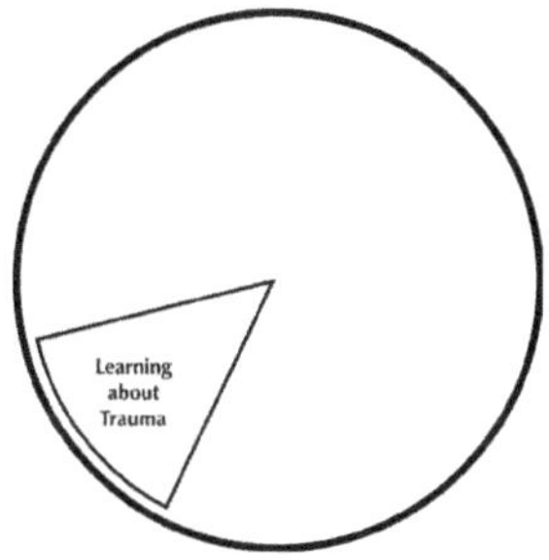


## LEARNING ABOUT TRAUMA

When I was diagnosed with multiple personality disorder in 1992 (renamed dissociative identity disorder in 1994), there was precious little support for people like me. Facebook didn't exist, so there were no Facebook support groups. The internet was new and mostly inaccessible, so researching the condition was hardly an option. I read books, but there were few available. Feeling isolated and alone, I lacked the capacity to learn more about my condition. For many years, all I knew about DID was what I experienced myself, and I often doubted what my own body, mind, and spirit were telling me.

It's been an eye-opener to discover the wealth of information and support that has grown over the past thirty years. When I was in the midst of my recovery, I thought, at times, that I was the only person in the world with DID. I thought it was a bizarre diagnosis, rare and uncommon. Actually, DID is not rare at all; it's estimated that 1–3 percent of people worldwide have either diagnosed or undiagnosed DID as the mind's natural response to unremitting childhood trauma. By comparison, bipolar disorder is estimated in 2.8 percent of the population and rising, which by some measures is called an epidemic.

Once I was diagnosed, I was sure that I was "doing it wrong." If I really had DID, I would display certain symptoms or experience certain kinds of situations. Instead, I was displaying other symptoms and experiencing other kinds of situations. I had no perspective except what was right in front of my nose. I needed, but hardly received, a knowledge base to support my recovery.

Janina Fisher refers to her first teacher, Judith Herman, who taught her that survivors need information. "They [need] to be educated about trauma and all its ramifications and manifestations. They [need] to know enough to make intelligent choices about their lives and treatment. . . . As victims of trauma, they [have] been disempowered and deprived of choice."[45]

So, survivors need to be full collaborators with the therapist rather than passive recipients of therapy, both Fisher and Herman conclude. "The antidote," Fisher writes, channeling Herman, is "the power of knowledge—some way to understand the baffling and intense reactions that [plague] them, often for years, so they [do] not feel so crazy and abnormal."[46] Both Fisher and Herman have provided a road map that shines a light on the path ahead. Other books, workshops, and peer support groups do the same.

In spite of the fact that we still need more trained therapists who understand dissociative disorders, the difference in capacity between then and now is astounding. Today, more therapists are ready to walk the walk into the dark corridors of a frightening past. Today, more therapists understand the full impact of trauma and share that knowledge with their clients. Today, fewer therapists are denying dissociative responses to trauma; they're willing to learn, not only from their professional resources, but from their clients who are the true experts.

The first step in comprehending our symptoms is to have a therapist who can illuminate what's happening to us, place it in context, and lead us forward. The next step is to gather all the information available about trauma, our diagnoses, and the variety of treatments. On the whole, people who use dissociation as a coping strategy tend to be bright and creative. (Yes, that means you!) Armed with information, recovery becomes an adventure into self-knowledge.

## EXERCISE 19: BUILD YOUR LIBRARY

**Go to the library and check out a book on the subject of trauma and healing. You can find some good ones in the endnotes of this book, or you can find your own. Read the book, as your system allows. Keep a record of the books you've read on trauma and healing below.**

## SEEKING JUSTICE

The word justice conjures up images of courtrooms, jail cells, and articulate lawyers. While some survivors are successful in bringing charges against their perpetrators and receiving some sort of legal justice, the vast majority of us simply don't have the courtroom evidence to go that mile. That doesn't mean, however, that we can't extract justice from the universe for the harms we've endured. Seeking justice, each in our own way, is an important part of our healing journey.

Like the words *healing* and *forgiving,* experts haven't always agreed on the definition of justice. From ancient times to the present day, philosophers and legal scholars have offered their understandings of the meaning of justice in a variety of contexts. Most people believe that justice is the quality of being impartial and fair, in conformity with what is morally upright or good. Regardless of the context, most definitions can be distilled to fairness, equal rights, and respect.

As survivors, we often use surrogates to attain justice. In other words, we find other people, causes, or situations on which we project a sense of rightness, even when we're still contending with the wrongness of our past. For instance, the writers who participate in Dissociative Writers writing workshops share their stories through writing and affirm each other as they claim their voices. Speaking truth and being affirmed is one way to claim justice. If others acknowledge the wrong that was done, we can reduce the impact of those who denied it and help create a universe that honors truth.

> *"As survivors, we often use surrogates to attain justice."*

British author Carolyn Spring wrote a memoir entitled *Recovery is My Best Revenge.*[47] Her title not only embodies the groundswell of the justified anger we carry, it proclaims justice as our very act of healing. We cannot change the past, nor can we erase the people who hurt us, but we can set whatever boundaries we may need in order to heal. Over time, the larger-than-life abuser shrinks into a pitiful shell of a person as we grow stronger, more sure of ourselves, and more capable of seeing the whole picture as the competent adults that we are. This is justice in its finest form.

Some survivors become therapists themselves in order to stand against abuse by helping other survivors. Their insight and compassion are gifts from the rubble and are irreplaceable in the therapy room. Other survivors start organizations that address trauma in unique and effective ways.

Spring founded a website called Reversing Adversity that offers insightful video classes for both survivors and therapists. Linda Crockett, founder of Safe Communities, began her work helping churches and other groups create safe spaces for children. Jaime Pollack, director of An Infinite Mind, founded one of the largest organizations for people with dissociative identity disorder. Judie is the creator of Survivors Speak Truth, a "living classroom" of ritual abuse survivors and therapists, which broadens therapeutic awareness to ensure survivors receive appropriate care. Kait Gannon, creator of the podcast, *The Ugly Truth About the Girl Next Door,* is founder of not only the podcast but a nonprofit called Mezzo that educates the public about family-controlled sex trafficking.

We can't all start organizations, but many of us can support or volunteer for them. Or we might become involved in a cause that has nothing to do with trauma, such as animal welfare, working with preschool children, or welcoming immigrants. These, too, are ways of seeking justice in the aftermath of an unjust past.

In the beginning of my recovery, a friend who was active in a twelve-step program encouraged me to give back as a way to enhance my recovery from chronic childhood trauma. My heart wanted to do what she suggested, but I only had the inner resources to survive and put one foot in front of the other. For many years, I had no excess energy to give to others. In fact, it was a huge learning curve just to take the time to give to myself. *What good would I be for others if I don't take care of myself first?* I thought. If you're not ready to seek justice through surrogates, that's okay. Your time will come. Someday you'll take one little step to stand up, speak up, or gear up for something bigger than you. In your own way, you'll find and spread the justice that we're all due.

As we work toward justice through our surrogate people, causes, and situations, we find meaning in our suffering and purpose for our living. Meaning and purpose are drivers in the healing process, transforming us into so much more than the hurts we carry. We slowly claim our inner strength because we can't escape from it, no matter what our old tapes tell us. We have meaning. We have purpose. We are making a difference. The world needs us. We need us. Because we seek justice, a little corner of the world becomes a better place.

## EXERCISE 20: DO SOMETHING GOOD

**Join Dissociative Writers, attend a Healing Together Conference with An Infinite Mind, or volunteer for an organization that does good in the world.[48] Keep a list of all the ways you help others, such as, "I foster rescued animals," or "I hold space for my sister." What does surrogate justice look like for you?**

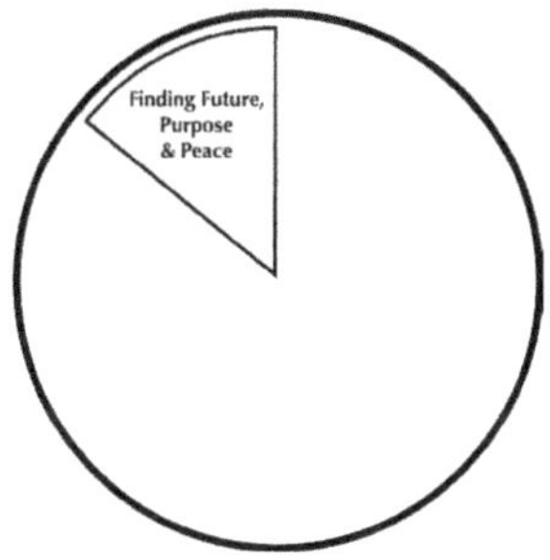


## FINDING FUTURE, PURPOSE & PEACE

We all come to our diagnoses at different places in our lives. Some of us are barely surviving and may be living on public assistance. Others of us may have a parent or a spouse who provides us with financial support and, if we're lucky, a soft landing. We may be working at jobs we love or jobs we hate, or we may not be able to manage a job at all. We may have big families, small families, or no families. Some of us may be in school or have successful careers. We may have big dreams or no dreams at all. We may burst with creativity in our chosen medium, or we may yearn to express ourselves but don't have the self-confidence or life circumstances to allow for it. Some of us may feel fully functional, with the added complexity of multiple selves; others of us may feel fully dysfunctional, with the added complexity of multiple selves; and others, still, may be somewhere in between. It's an understatement to say that no two of us are alike, and our multiplicity manifests in unique ways.

Everyone, however, has to find a way to fit the work I've described in this chapter into the doldrums, the doubt, the inspiration, the joy, the confusion, the chaos, the successes, the rewards, the highs, and the lows of everyday life. In the early years of your recovery, you may be fully focused on the work before you. It may consume you, confound you, and connect you with yourself or selves, leading you deeper into your psyche and further along your journey. As I've noted before, you will get to know who you are better than most people. Yes, it hurts to know yourself, but it also helps, and eventually it molds you into the person you were meant to be.

There comes a point in your work—maybe gradually or maybe suddenly—when you realize you have more space to grow, more energy to expend, and more love to give. In spite of—and maybe because of—the hard life you've lived and the healing work you've traveled, you bask in rewards you weren't expecting and possibilities you dared not dream. The fruits of your labor are the future you are living here and now.

Building your future and finding peace is the culmination of cycling through the Healing Wheel many times over while using your healing intention as your guide. You are more than your symptoms, so who will you be without the fear, shame, triggers, and identity confusion—when the marks of trauma are no longer front and center?

You are coming home. Taste it. Breathe it in. Look around and take it in. It's almost in reach.

Keep cycling!

> *"There comes a point in your work—maybe gradually or maybe suddenly—when you will realize you have more space to grow, more energy to expend, and more love to give."*

## EXERCISE 21: DEFINING PEACE

**Peace is a fluid word that has many meanings. What does peace look like to you, both now and in the future? Do you experience peace in the present? What are the characteristics of the peace you will achieve in the future?**

## JAIME MICHELLE'S STORY

Jaime is the founder of an organization dedicated to survivors with dissociative identity disorder called An Infinite Mind. AIM holds a popular annual conference called Healing Together. In her "other" life, Jaime is an educator who has taught in the classroom and serves as a district resource coach. She's also a happy wife and a nurturing mother to many furry animals. She is childless (externally) by choice.

In high school, Jaime became aware that she was moving through life in a robotic fashion, numb and disconnected from her peers. She felt different from her classmates and didn't know why. This sense of disconnection continued into college when she began to have anxiety, panic attacks, and nightmares. Jaime began to see a therapist, and over the course of ten years, she was diagnosed with many other disorders until she landed in the office of a therapist who understood the symptoms Jaime was experiencing.

While previous therapists seemed intent on pigeonholing Jaime into more acceptable diagnoses like schizophrenia, schizoaffective disorder, or bipolar disorder, the new mental health provider saw something different in her, and she was diagnosed with DID shortly thereafter. Her healing work included modalities like hypnotherapy, art therapy, play therapy, and EMDR (eye movement desensitization and reprocessing). "It wasn't linear," she said, "more spiral, with two steps forward and one step back. It wasn't easy." Today, Jaime has completed the bulk of her healing work and considers herself functionally multiple. As many readers are aware, Jaime has sought justice on the Healing Wheel by building an organization that eases suffering for others and creates space to learn, connect, and bond.

Jaime was abused by two family members who never made amends for the harm they caused. She believes that forgiveness is for someone who is sorry, contrite, and makes amends—and her abusers don't qualify. "Forgiveness is a special gift I have to offer. It's not for myself, it's for them. My abusers don't deserve that gift." She understands that her abusers were both complicated people and were probably abused themselves, and she can empathize with their situations to some extent. But, "they didn't earn the gift of my forgiveness. That's the natural consequence of their actions."

# 7

## MANY REWARDS

*Pain is transformed into wisdom.*

"Thank you for talking with me," said the lady in the blue dress who sat in the front pew of the church I served each Sunday morning. "I don't know how I'd manage without your wisdom. I'm much too confused to know how to proceed." She was newly widowed and overwhelmed by life circumstances. I was happy to offer her pastoral counseling as she confronted her grief and the new normal that was thrust upon her.

Years before, this very same woman would have been an object of my envy. She had everything, or so it seemed. While I was crawling through the muck and mud of my life, she was living in a big house and vacationing in exotic places. While I could barely make ends meet, she wore designer clothes. While I had no friends, she was surrounded by adoring people.

How could it be that I was the one who was helping her? That she was looking up to me in her time of need? That I was clearly the more resilient person in the room at this moment in time? I had lost my fantasy childhood and was abandoned and disowned by my parents. I lost two marriages, one to emotional abuse and divorce, the other to death. The idyllic childhood I had hoped to provide for my own children was a wisp in the wind. In the midst of all this, another world of body memories, fear, isolation, and parts of myself permeated every corner of my being, rendering me incapacitated at times.

Who would have thought that the work of the Healing Wheel would carry me through the storm and land me on the other side as a mentor, a person with wisdom? Indeed, this very same work will do the same for you. You will emerge from this hell of healing as a person with strength and character. Others will turn to you in need. Exercising your boundaries, you will help as you can and point them forward as they embark on their own healing path.

There are many rewards you'll collect along your journey. For me, gratitude, compassion, and a sense of something more were just a few.

## GRATITUDE

"Gratitude?" I asked. "What's that?" My head was spinning from my chaotic life. I couldn't keep my balance and was holding on by a thin thread. Friends in my faith community talked about gratitude as if it were a required ingredient in a favorite recipe and as abundant as an old-fashioned pump flowing like water. Gratitude, you say? What do I have to be grateful for?

I suspect that many people who dissociate as a primary coping strategy have times in their lives when they feel like I did. You don't have to have a dissociative disorder to run into uphill battles regarding jobs, living situations, children, lovers, and more. That's just life, and it's tough. But when you add onto that the profound losses, devastating memories, and unrelenting pain that survivors of chronic childhood abuse experience, it's understandable that we aren't likely to have a lot of space for gratitude.

Yet gratitude may be the first sign that your healing journey is gaining ground, that it's working, that it's having an impact on your life. Like a seed that sprouts small shoots, one at a time, gratitude comes slowly, in small doses. You might miss this new development if you don't look carefully with lenses that are grounded in reality. Often my life was a checkerboard where small spots of gratitude were interspersed between larger swaths of pain. Regardless of the difficulties you might be going through, there's something liberating in becoming aware of the one or two things that are good in your life.

Gratitude is unlikely to be a driving force in early recovery—if it is, you may be in denial, pretending all is well when it's not. Instead, the early stages of healing make it hard to see the forest for the trees. When you begin the work of healing, your forest is cluttered with trees, filled with work, scattered with uncertainty. Coming face-to-face with your history and how it manifests in your present-day life is more than enough for anyone to manage. It's okay, then, to forget about being thankful in the beginning of your recovery because there's not much to be thankful for.

As the fog clears slowly over time, though, as you begin to breathe in the person you are becoming, as you embody your healing, you'll become more and more grateful for what you experience that is good. Not all of life is bad, not everyone is evil, not every slight is intentional. In the muck and mess of life, there's room to be grateful for a therapist who walks into dark places with you, for friends you can count on, for family members who deserve your trust, for greater strength and resilience, for new wisdom, for new opportunities, for new love, for the life you live, and for the air you breathe.

> *"Like a seed that sprouts small shoots, one at a time, gratitude comes slowly, in small doses."*

After years of feeling unsafe, our friend Sharri finds she's grateful that she's safe and has recovered from much of her past trauma. "I'm thankful for the people God has put in my life to help me along the way, especially for my husband, who was the first person to really love me." Judie has a difficult time with gratitude because of all her losses, yet she can still say, "I am grateful to God I'm alive." I can't tell you how many people have told me how grateful they are for Dissociative Writers because it has brought them together with other survivors.

Over the course of your healing, you will discover what keeps you going, what breathes life into your body, what makes you smile and laugh, what makes you stretch and strive, what helps you rest and renew, what makes you happy and sad, and even what makes you cry. Authentically feeling all of your emotions drives your behavior and is the stuff of gratitude, which is the foundation of your *whole life*. Gratitude will come—in its own time.

## COMPASSION

". . . and that's the way it is."

Jenna finished reading her poem about a rocky relationship that was sucking the life out of her. Suddenly the Zoom screen was covered with hearts rising from the fifteen black boxes that held the faces of participants in this Dissociative Writers workshop. The reaction button at the bottom of the screen offered everyone the opportunity to give instant feedback. The other writers knew the meaning of Jenna's poem. They understood her pain at a deep level. They had been there and done that. The facilitator asked them to give Jenna oral feedback and, one by one, their comments expressed not only thoughts about the poem itself, but also compassion about the angst it embodied.

I haven't met all the dissociative people in the world, but the ones I have met are filled with compassion. We have a special sensitivity toward others who may be suffering, especially those with backgrounds similar to ours. My heart is warmed when my peers relate with kindness to others who've shared their stories. In safe spaces like writing, art, and community workshops, we can affirm, support, and even forgive others who are vulnerable like us.

At the same time, I'm sure our compassion is not a linear achievement. We may be triggered by others, or we may shut out people who remind us of our past. Sometimes our protectors may lash out in anger when, indeed, the situation calls for patience, understanding, or kindness. At other times, we simply don't have the energy to feel compassion toward others when every ounce of our own reserves goes into surviving. These are normal responses to the abuse we suffered. It may take years of engaging in the work of healing to open up pathways of compassion for others.

> *"We have a special sensitivity toward others who may be suffering, especially those with backgrounds similar to ours."*

As with forgiveness, the most important person we need to show compassion toward is ourselves. You may remember Michael, whom we met in an earlier chapter, who found it easier to feel compassion for his familial abuser than to show compassion for himself. Yet he understands that he, too, deserves compassion for the suffering he endured. Perhaps, in some cases, showing compassion to others is a rehearsal for applying the same grace to the wounded parts of ourselves.

An unexpected surprise that may emerge in the final stages of healing when we are building a future and finding peace is a sense of compassion for our perpetrators. Bonnie's long road to healing, summarized earlier, was contingent on growing her "compassion muscle" for her perpetrators. She built a bonfire to consume the male organ that had hurt her and, in so doing, saw her perps' pain rise with the smoke. When reflecting on the impact that ritual had on her healing, she notes that forgiving the pain they caused was impossible, but compassion for the pain they endured was crucial.

Feeling compassion is not the same as forgiving. It's understanding the context in which our abusers lost touch with their humanity and succumbed to their suffering by hurting others. When we have healed most aspects of our woundedness, we may be ready to see those who hurt us as people who have been hurt too. This in no way excuses them. Nor does it mean we've forgiven them. It only means we understand—at least in a small way—why they may have done what they've done.

"I've released them," Bonnie concludes.

## SPIRITUALITY

"People who believe in God are either stupid or weak." I quoted these words of my father in my memoir.[49] For him and everyone else in my family, God did not exist, "something greater than" was a phrase used in mathematics, and reality was reduced to what you could see, hear, touch, taste, or feel. Spirituality in any form was not just discouraged but quashed.

"You don't want to be stupid or weak, do you, Popup?" He badgered me with this question, using my baby name, until our atheism became the calling card that said we were a family who was smart and strong. It was a long road for me to create my own calling card separate from my family, but, gradually, my spirituality discovered me; it seemed to follow me around like a puppy demanding to be acknowledged and fed.

Many people think spirituality means religion and the trappings that come with belief systems, houses of worship, and ministries, but I believe that it is much more. Instead, I think of it as the awareness of a mystery that lives within ourselves and beyond ourselves, an awareness that makes us more than ourselves, more than our pain, more than our chaos, and, likewise, more than our gifts and accomplishments.

When we can manage a trigger in the morning and volunteer at a homeless shelter in the afternoon, that's a sign of a resilient spirituality where our wounds are healed by the compassion we show to others. When we can't remember anything that happened the day before but can frolic in a field of daisies the day after, that's a sign of a joyful spirituality where we delight in spite of our limitations. We have lived much of our lives with the mystery of our multiple selves; why can't we live with the mystery of something more?

Ronald Rolheiser, author of *The Holy Longing*, quotes Plato as saying, "We are fired into life with a madness from the gods."[50] Consequently, he says, everyone has a spirituality, everyone has a fire we are born with; it's what we do with that fire that directs who we become. We can turn it inward and become a couch potato who is bitter and depressed (not to be confused with our righteous anger and wells of deep grief), and that's our spirituality: a survivor who is stuck in the mire of a problematic past. Or, we can use our time to meditate or create art or help another person, and that's our spirituality: a survivor who is sending good vibes into the world even if our own world needs some cleaning up. Our angst may limit how we embody our spirituality during the most difficult periods of our lives, but, as we grow, we have more space to be true to our own spirits.

Sometimes, but not always, spirituality *is* connected to religion. I am a faithful Christian, but I'm careful not to define spirituality in the way that I experience it, because you may experience it differently. Your spirit may claim Judaism, Islam, paganism, or another organized system of understanding the world within and without and beyond. Or, you may embrace some of the core values of religion but look to the universe as your mandala. Or, you may reject religion altogether and claim another worldview that makes space for you to flourish so you know there is mystery somewhere in the mix of your experience.

Aces was raised a Christian with wide parameters because their mother exposed them to the views of many world religions. Over time and not without struggle, they discovered they had metaphysical gifts that led them to shamanism, specifically a form that derives from indigenous peoples in the Andes Mountains known as the Q'ero. In that context, they engaged in various forms of energy work, including soul retrieval, and have found that this expression of spirituality has a tremendous impact on their healing. In their belief system, when someone has been traumatized, a piece of their soul breaks off and must be reunited to be healed. Aces has found soul retrieval to be instrumental in the healing of alters, memories, and triggers, including reuniting with alters when soul pieces return. These experiences inspired Aces to study shamanism and perform soul retrieval with other DID systems.

Regardless of where the "fire in the belly" leads, it's an important part of becoming who we are and knowing our place in the universe. Our spirituality reminds us that we matter. Overcoming our shame, finding our voice, healing our wounds, and living into our deepest longings, together with other good people, is the purpose of life. The mystery of spirit invites us to embrace the whisper, "I love you," when we're scared and alone, it marvels at the breeze that tickles our skin when walking in nature, and it integrates the wisdom we are learning now into the person we will be in the future.

These surprises are meant to be pondered as we embrace our spirituality as a force that lifts us into another plane, enabling us to live into our intention and become the person that we are meant to be.

*"Our spirituality reminds us that we matter."*

## EXERCISE 22: WISDOM WAYS

**In what ways are you wiser today than you were before you started your healing journey? Do gratitude, compassion, and spirituality factor into your wisdom? Or does your wisdom take other forms or shapes? Write about your wisdom, in whatever form it takes, here:**

## LYN'S STORY

Lyn's story—yes, that's me! I've already told a good portion of my story in my memoir, and you've gotten a taste of it here and there throughout this book. I'll recap a little of the trajectory of my healing here.

I grew up in an unusually isolated family on the edge of Philadelphia in a second-floor apartment overlooking Rte. 1 Baltimore Pike with my mother, father, sister, and brother. In my earliest years, my paternal grandparents lived with us too. I always sensed we were a strange family under the iron-fisted hand of my father, and I suspected I was defective, too, but wasn't sure what that meant. In spite of my social paralysis, I managed to meet and marry a man who was my husband for twenty years, and together we created four beautiful children.

Although everyone in my family thought we were the perfect couple, including me, the revelation of my husband's affairs was the stimulus for my hidden system to emerge and break apart. The carefully cultivated garden of my family disintegrated into a rubble consisting of my husband's rage, my children's fear, and my incompetent victimhood. I huddled into corners and hung on for dear life. To be honest, as much as I loved my children, I clearly was unable to parent them effectively during this time.

An ugly divorce, chaotic internal chaos, a thirty-day hospital stay, and a suicide attempt eventually landed me the diagnosis of dissociative identity disorder. I had no narrative memories of abuse but was consumed by body memory and elusive fragments. My father tried to dissuade me from exploring the "hobgoblins" of the past, and he otherwise tried to sabotage my recovery. When my mother disowned me, I grasped at that get-out-of-jail-free card and embraced the estrangement to embark on a ten-year recovery path.

To summarize my agonizing journey toward healing into a few words, I plumbed my depths, met more than twenty alters, learned to love them, and integrated. That's where my memoir ends. After the publication of *Crazy*, my daughter's anguished response prompted my system to fragment again; several alters reappeared and two new alters emerged. Decades ago, I had overpowering emotions but no narrative. Today, as I've picked up my work again, I have narrative but no emotion. Our brains and bodies are pretty amazing things—it's taken thirty years for me to integrate the two!

Throughout the worst of my timeline, I never thought about forgiving my abusers. All my energy was directed toward surviving. As I've healed, that inner resistance to forgiving has continued. Like Sharon, I don't hate my parents, but neither do I love them. They are simply a part of a story that happened in my past, who exist, in my mind, without emotion. Instead, I choose to live a happy, healthy life surrounded by positive relationships and fulfilling activities, made possible only by my commitment to deep work.

I felt compassion for both my father and my mother when they died, I am buoyed by a deep faith denied to me when I was young, and—having suffered—I am grateful for every breath I take and for life itself. Living a whole life is of the "ground of my being"[51]; forgiving is not.

# 8

# COMING HOME

*A whole life is the ultimate reward.*

"The integration of my alters into my whole self was never in question," I wrote in my memoir,[52] drawing from journal entries more than two decades earlier. The closing chapter described the gentle integration of twenty or so parts who chose, on their own, to function as one.

"They will always be there," I wrote, "because that's the way my brain was formed in those developmental, traumatic years of my life. They did their work, and now we were one."[53]

My musings were prescient because, back in those days, I didn't know much about how the brain protects the child from trauma, and even less about integration and what that meant. The only word I had been exposed to that described healing from dissociative identity disorder was *integration*, and the only vision for wholeness was becoming one. Today there are a whole host of words and visions: integration, fusion, final fusion, unification, functional multiplicity, and more. Sometimes, people try to hammer out hard-and-fast definitions for each of these, but often our lived experience defies being put in a box.

For twenty years after my integration, I lived a whole life. It was not a perfect life, and I certainly had more healing to accomplish, but I was integrated and whole, living as one. Yet after I published my memoir, my system split apart again. This time around, some new insiders made themselves known, and some of the original ones resurfaced. We continued the work of healing where we had left off.

Some would say that I was integrated and a stressor caused my split. In this scenario, I would eventually integrate again as one. Others would say I was and am functionally multiple at the same time that I'm integrated and share knowledge between alters. We tend to put *integration* and *functional multiplicity* into two separate camps, but I wonder if this is a false dichotomy. I've written about this elsewhere,[54] but the point is that the language we use is never precise even as it describes the experiences we carry.

How I understood integration then is different from the way I understand it today, just as assimilating functional multiplicity into my vocabulary reshapes my understanding of all the other healing words for dissociation.

> *"Language, perhaps, is the key to unlocking the tension between healing and forgiving."*

The same may be true for the words *healing* and *forgiving.* The way you and I understand these two powerful words is influenced by our experiences. The language we use is limited by our observations, our triggers, our emotions, our beliefs, our failures, our successes, our hopes, our dreams, and the ongoing trajectory of our lives. Language, perhaps, is the key to unlocking the tension between healing and forgiving.

## THE LANGUAGE WE USE

Because you are a one-of-a-kind human being, your journey is unique, your responses are unique, and the language you use to describe your experiences is unique. Take, for instance, Jayden, a survivor of ritual abuse and mind control, as they reflect on the word forgiveness while asking these questions:

> *What needs and emotions are we trying to express through the word* forgiveness*? Are there other words we could use as a culture instead? Is* forgiveness *a word that's been imposed on us, and should we be looking for a word that conveys similar needs and emotions? Or is it still a useful word?*

It's remarkable to me how people who describe their healing journeys in similar ways may use different words. Two people may have done the hard work described in this book and more and have come to a place in their healing where they've found a sense of peace. One person may use the word forgiveness in that equation and one person may not. We've seen Sharri, whose belief system prompted her desire to forgive as a part of her healing. We've also seen Gabby, who has no interest in forgiving her perpetrator whatsoever. Both—along with every other survivor we've met in this workbook—are working hard to write new endings to their stories.

Recently, about a dozen Dissociative Writers gathered to talk about the role forgiveness does or does not play in their healing process. As you might expect, all of them wanted to reach a place of peace—in the words of the hero's journey, to "come home"—and some of them already had. Yet for most, the word forgiveness was anathema to their journey. They proposed, instead, that we use language such as disentanglement, un-enmeshment, severing of connections, reclaiming and/or owning power, releasing, breaking trauma bonds, accepting, letting go, changing heart, and cultivating compassion when talking about their hopes for their healing.

These are descriptive words that aren't loaded like the word forgiveness. They aren't used as pressure points for people who have been victims at the hands of others. They don't expect positive feelings toward the perpetrator or giving gifts to demonstrate commitment. They honor the integrity of the wounded person to choose the path that is right for them, whether that may be to add forgiveness to one's own personal vocabulary, or to strike the word from any accounting. They are the words that any mythic hero might use toward the journey's end.

The language you use reflects your beliefs, your values, and your history. You can heal from chronic childhood trauma using the language that works for you. You are a hero, and coming home earns you the right to choose.

## EXERCISE 23: CLAIMING YOUR LANGUAGE

**Is *forgiveness* the word you would use to describe the peace you're working toward? Are there other words you might use instead of or in addition to it? Can you add to the list made by the Dissociative Writers focus group? Make a list of words or phrases that make sense to you.**

## THE JOURNEY CHANGES BUT NEVER ENDS

The journey to a whole life changes, but it never ends.

As you cycle through the Healing Wheel and embody your healing intention—over the course of years, even decades—your confidence will grow and your pain will diminish. You'll know who you are, and you'll love yourself or your selves. You'll feel all your feelings without numbing or disappearing, and you'll know how to navigate any triggers that crop up. You'll create a new normal from the rubble of your traumatic past, and you'll have the energy to follow through on your passions. You'll have a life, a community, a purpose, and a sense of peace. Your history may have shaped you, but your courage will define you.

Most likely, you'll learn to forgive your friends and family members who have proven themselves to be trustworthy when they occasionally stumble and step on your toes. And you'll learn to ask for their forgiveness when you do the same. For most of us, forgiving ourselves is a never-ending journey, so you'll probably continue to work on being as compassionate to yourself as you are to other people. You'll embrace intimacy and the risks and joys that come with it.

If forgiving your perpetrators is important to you, however you define the word, then you'll probably cross that goal line. If forgiving perpetrators isn't on your to-do list, you'll feel a sense of acceptance and peace regardless. The difference between forgiving and healing is less important to you now because your healing has led you to a whole life.

> *"You are a work of art that is more beautiful because of the wisdom that's grown out of your wounds."*

Will your life be perfect? Probably not. The truth is that no one's life is perfect, even the people who look like they have everything together. Once we are integrated, functionally multiple, or both, we'll continue to navigate the ups and downs of life, but we'll do it with more clarity and less confusion. Healing is a lifelong journey for everyone—you are a step ahead of people without trauma histories because you have delved more deeply into your darkness to transform your wounds into wisdom. Like the Japanese kintsugi art form that repairs cracked pottery with gold, leaving the piece more beautiful than before the ruptures, you are a work of art that is more beautiful because of the wisdom that's grown out of your wounds.

Some of that beauty comes in the form of surprise benefits that you weren't expecting when you first began your healing journey. In the beginning, you just wanted to survive, you wanted your pain to go away, you wanted a sense of coherency to your life. As you move further along that journey, you discover more than you knew how to imagine. Gratitude, compassion, spirituality, and other gifts are a part of the kaleidoscope that shines through your broken places.

## REVISITING YOUR HEALING INTENTION

Now is the time to revisit your healing intention.

You may not be home yet, but your intention is your vision for what home will look like. That vision may be consistent throughout the decades of your healing, or it may change based on the way *you* change.

Change, in this case, is growth. Your journey around the Healing Wheel is growing you emotionally, mentally, behaviorally, and spiritually. Growth is always uneven, so don't be discouraged if you take two steps forward and one back, or if you sometimes feel as if you're spinning around in the same place. In our fast-paced, disposable society, it's easy to forget that all good things take time. Maybe that's why it's called a hero's journey. You are moving, inch by inch, step by step, toward the home you envision for yourself, and that takes the indomitable spirit of a hero.

It's natural, even desirable, to make changes to your intention based on the stirrings of your heart and mind. Reflect often. Revise as needed. This is your road map that will lead you to your destination.

> *"Your journey around the Healing Wheel is growing you emotionally, mentally, behaviorally, and spiritually."*

Who will you be? What a wonderful question to ask yourself! You have the power, now, to shape yourself in ways you never could before. Will you live alone or have a companion? Will you have a job that fulfills you or a creative expression that completes you? Have your parts integrated into a unified whole, or will they remain functionally multiple as they embrace life? Feel free to revise your intention any number of times as you grow and learn and change. Your intention is the blueprint for your future, and the more you internalize it—post it on your refrigerator, look at it, read it, shout it from the rooftop—the more your selves will lead you to your destination.

## EXERCISE 24: REVISITING YOUR HEALING INTENTION

**As you reread your intention for healing, remember that it's your vision for your future, your purpose, your manifestation of home. Does it embody all you imagine home to be? Do you need to change it? If so, rewrite it here to better express your intention. If you are satisfied with it, transfer it to a document that you can hang in your safe space as a reminder of your destination.**

## YOU ARE THE HERO

If you're like many of us, you're uncomfortable with compliments. They may feel dangerous or seductive. They may feel inflated or untrue. You may not trust them, so you try to deflect them. The old tapes may keep you captive to the old narrative. So when I tell you that you are the hero of your own story, you may not believe me.

Regardless, I am here to tell you that YOU ARE THE HERO!

Looking through a mythic lens, heroes tend to be humble people who accept new challenges as they arise. Inwardly, they may doubt their capacity to overcome obstacles, but outwardly, they meet each obstacle head-on, one step at a time. On occasion, heroes may walk away from what's in front of them, but they learn soon enough that avoidance doesn't solve the problem, so they turn back and look the tiger in the eye. Heroes are not out for accolades; they want to fulfill a purpose that, at the outset, they may not be able to articulate themselves. An inner drive urges them forward, sometimes in spite of the hero's resistance. After finding mentors, enduring tests, and overcoming almost insurmountable odds, the hero returns home with new wisdom and a peaceful sense of courage.

You may buy this description for Dorothy in *The Wizard of Oz*, or Odysseus in *The Odyssey*, or Luke Skywalker in *Star Wars*. But you may not see yourself in this narrative. Give yourself some time, and you will discover your true grit—the fire in your belly that leads you home.

> *"You are the hero!"*

## EXERCISE 25: THE HERO'S JOURNEY

**Below is the narration of the hero, in the hero's journey, with names and pronouns left out. Try adding your own name in the first open space, using first-person pronouns in the rest of the text. Allow yourself to claim your identity as a hero.**

**Or, try adding your own name but use second- or third-person pronouns, as if someone else is talking about you. Use plural pronouns if that's how you naturally refer to yourself.**

**Reread the narrative. How does it feel to claim the well-deserved honor of "hero"? How does it feel to hear someone else talk about you in this way?**

__________ tends to be a humble person who accepts new challenges as they arise. Inwardly, __________ may doubt __________ capacity to overcome obstacles, but outwardly, __________ meet(s) each obstacle head-on, one step at a time. On occasion, __________ may walk away from what's in front of __________, but __________ learn(s) soon enough that avoidance doesn't solve the problem, so __________ turn(s) back and look(s) the tiger in the eye. __________ is not out for accolades; __________ want(s) to fulfill a purpose that, at the outset, __________ may not be able to articulate her/him/them(self/selves). An inner drive urges __________ forward, sometimes in spite of __________ resistance. After finding mentors, enduring tests, and overcoming almost insurmountable odds, __________ returns home with new wisdom and a peaceful sense of courage.

## COMING HOME

Coming home to the place where you began, but knowing it for the first time, is worthy of celebration. Cycling through the Healing Wheel using your intention as your guide is the backdrop for your success. You deserve to revel in your accomplishment. You are the hero of your own story!

But don't get complacent. Life, with or without trauma, is a journey. For an experienced hero like you, new challenges and new opportunities are inevitable. You will pick up the mantle again to climb mountains and conquer dragons. While all journeys can be difficult, frightening, and confusing, they can also be rewarding, exhilarating, and fulfilling if you approach them with your full self and all that you've learned along the way. In a very real sense, *you* are your destination. Each step into the unknown will lead you to a deeper appreciation of the home that exists in you.

Helen Keller wrote, "Life is either a daring adventure or nothing. To keep our faces toward change and behave like free spirits in the presence of fate is strength undefeatable."[55]

May you embrace your journey as the adventure that leads you home.

## EXERCISE 26: PLANNING YOUR PARTY!

**With the Healing Wheel as your map and your healing intention as your destination, paint a picture—using words or art or music—of the day you arrive home. Describe your *whole life*. Does it match your healing intention, or is it different? If different, how so? What does it look like? How do you feel? Who is there? Take the time to imagine how you will celebrate. You've worked hard, and you deserve it!**

# APPENDIX A

# FOR CHRISTIANS WHO HAVE BEEN TAUGHT TO FORGIVE

If you are Christian, you may have been taught that you must forgive if you want God to forgive you. Scripture may have been used to prove that point. You may believe that forgiving is your only route to salvation, as difficult as that task may seem to be. You may be under the impression that forgiving is your responsibility with or without the participation of the person(s) who harmed you.

Reinterpretation of the scripture by biblical scholars Maria Mayo and Susannah Griffith may qualify what you've been taught. Both scholars show in detail that, in the Gospels, repentance on the part of the offender was required before the offended offered forgiveness. Moreover, forgiveness was less a matter of healing the offended, and more a matter of keeping the community together. Therefore, repentance of the sinner was expected; without it, the sinner was removed from the community and the person who was harmed was freed from the expectation to forgive.

Griffith interprets repentance as accountability. "In Hebrew, [repentance] is *yeshivah*, from the Hebrew root *shuv*. *Shuv* connotes a noticeable, tangible turn. A turn from darkness to light. A turn from sin to salvation. A turn from death to life."[56] Hence, when Jesus called for repentance from the offender in Luke 17: 3–4, he established that forgiveness rested on accountability.

Mayo categorizes all the passages related to forgiveness as either 1) direct instructions to forgive, 2) pronouncements of forgiveness, 3) warnings about the unforgivable sin, and 3) the prayer for forgiveness from the cross (see graphic 3).[57] Focusing primarily on direct instructions, she notes that in each passage listed there is some reference to repentance in the verses themselves or in the passages leading up to or after the forgiveness passage. For instance, in Luke 17:3–4, "If a brother or sister sins, you must rebuke the offender, and if there is repentance, you must forgive" (NRSVue). In Matthew 6: 9–13, The Lord's Prayer, Mayo interprets the first clause, "forgive us our debts," (NRSVue) as an acknowledgment of sin, repentance, and a need for forgiveness.[58] Finally, in John 23:34a, Jesus's cry from the cross, Mayo suggests that Jesus did not, himself, offer forgiveness, but prayed to the Father for mercy for his perpetrators.

It may be helpful to note that both Mayo and Griffith were victims of violence. "As a young woman, I was nearly killed by an intruder who broke into my home early one Sunday morning,"[59] explains Mayo in the introduction to her book. Griffith's young adulthood was marred by the domestic violence of her husband and father of her young children. Griffith did, eventually, forgive her husband from whom she was divorced, but only with his repentance and after a long process of discernment through scripture and community.

From another perspective, Christians may find comfort in experiencing God's grace in the healing process, which may ultimately lead to forgiving a perpetrator. Friar Peter Chepaitis, a Franciscan priest, notes that you never hear Jesus say, "I forgive you." Instead, his words are always a description of a gift already offered, as in "Your sins are forgiven."

Friar Peter says, "When someone comes to me and says, 'I can't forgive the person who hurt me or abused me,' my first response is, 'Of course you can't because forgiveness is always God's work.' Then I compare the process of forgiveness to the first three steps of Alcoholics Anonymous. As one recovering person once told me, they can be summarized as 'I can't. You, God, can. I think I'll let You.'"

Friar Peter affirms the psychologists previously mentioned who say that forgiving does not mean excusing the abuse. The evil of abuse must be rejected, he says. One way to heal from abuse is to name and reject the evil while letting God judge the person. He suggests that each individual may substitute another word for God, such as Jesus, Higher Power, Holy Spirit, Allah, or any other name that represents the divine for the person praying.[60]

## Graphic 2

**FORGIVENESS IN THE GOSPEL**

Adapted from *The Limits of Forgiveness: Case Studies in the Distortion of a Biblical Ideal* by Maria Mayo, 2015

| | **Matthew** | **Mark** | **Luke** | **John** |
|---|---|---|---|---|
| **1. Direct instructions to forgive** | 6:9-13 (the Lord's Prayer) | | 11:2-4 | |
| | 6:14-15 (forgive others in order to be forgiven by God) | 11:25 | 6:37-38 | 20:22-23 |
| | 18:21-22 (forgive seventy-seven times) | | 17:3-4 (if there is repentance you must forgive; forgive seven times) | |
| | 18:23-35 (parable of the unforgiving servant) | | | |
| **2. Pronounce-ments of forgiveness** | 9:2-8 (the healing of the paralyzed man) | 2:2-12 | 5:17-26 | |
| | | | 7:36-50 (a woman's sins have been forgiven) | |
| **3. Warnings about the unforgiveable sin** | 12:32 | | 3:29 | 12:10 |
| **4. The prayer for forgiveness from the cross** | | | 23:34a | |

# APPENDIX B

# TRAUMA AND THE BRAIN

Bessel van der Kolk, Janina Fisher, and many others describe at length the way the brain reacts when perceiving danger. For the purposes of this workbook, I offer a simplified explanation.

The front brain, or more specifically the prefrontal cortex, or thinking brain, is the place of higher-level cognition, decision-making, and narrative memory. This is the brain that dominates our conscious everyday living.

The back brain is made up of two systems that are activated in dangerous emergencies: the limbic system, also called the mammalian brain, and the brain stem, also called the reptilian brain. The limbic system moderates emotions with the front brain, acting as a bridge between feelings and cognition. The brain stem sends signals into the body to regulate bodily functions.

When faced with perceived danger, the amygdala, which is a part of the limbic system, sounds an alarm, and the brain stem reacts instinctively by mobilizing the body to take immediate action. For a few moments, the front brain is offline, unable to make rational decisions. Instead, the back brain marshals the troops throughout the body to protect the person in harm's way.

This finely tuned system has an evolutionary advantage. Imagine a landslide begins to fall all around you. Or a ferocious tiger is racing toward you. Or an angry stranger is heading your way. The back brain's impulse to run, climb, hide, or otherwise take cover propels you instantaneously and saves you from certain death. Had you taken the time to weigh your options with your front brain, you'd be buried beneath a pile of rocks, beaten to a pulp, or mauled to death. You survived because that's exactly how your back brain has evolved—to save you when you're threatened. Analyzing what happened and rethinking how you might avoid the situation in the future is the function of the front brain at a later time when you're out of danger. In the moment, the back brain saves the day.

In the here and now, your brain continues to serve this purpose when real danger threatens or when some stimulus reminds you of a past danger that no longer exists. This explains why trauma survivors often live in a back brain loop with body memories, emotional overload, and numbness—because current circumstances trigger the back brain's survival response. It also explains why many traumatic memories reside in the body rather than in the front brain. In the words of van der Kolk, "the body keeps the score."

Graphic 3

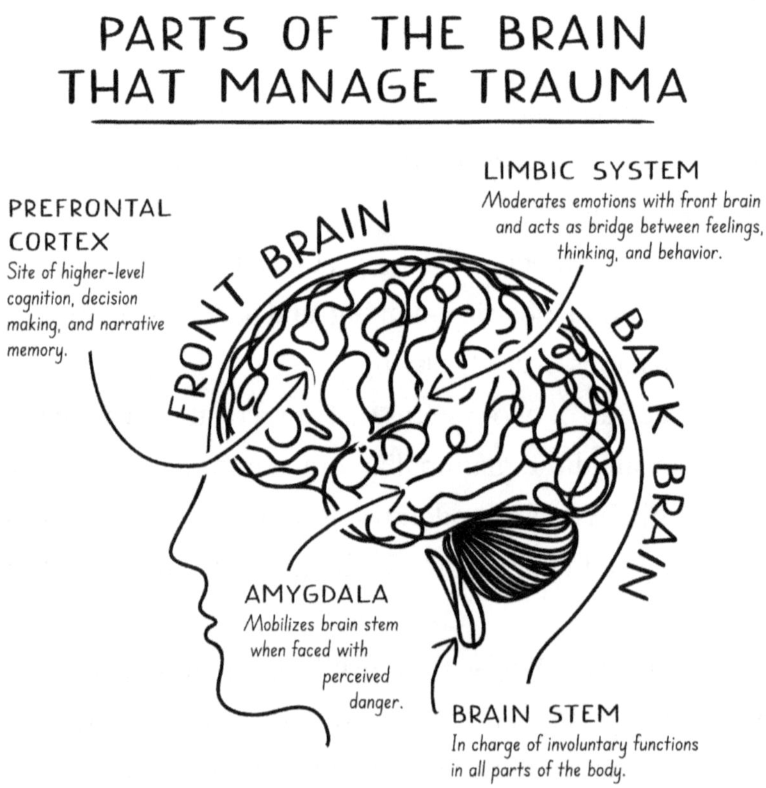

# APPENDIX C

Dissociative Writers, Inc. are people just like you and me—men, women, and nonbinary people who write about their experiences of living with a dissociative disorder using poetry, memoir, fiction, nonfiction, dramatic scripts, or whatever their chosen medium may be. We gather in virtual writers' workshops and in memoir classes to explore our creative depths through writing. We write at home, at work, in journals, on computers. We welcome our parts, young and old, to participate. We are a nonprofit whose mission is to provide a safe space to support one another in our writing as survivors and people with dissociative disorders, and to encourage the creativity that helped us survive to tell our stories.

For more information about Dissociative Writers, go to www.dissociativewriters.com.

# ENDNOTES

1 See Jamie Marich, *Dissociation Made Simple* (North Atlantic Books, 2023) for an in-depth discussion of how dissociation is experienced by different people.

2 Cathryn L. Taylor, *The Inner Child Workbook: What to Do with Your Past When It Just Won't Go Away* (Tarcher Press, 1991).

3 Richard Schwartz, *The Internal Family Systems Workbook: A Guide to Discover Your Self and Heal Your Parts* (Sounds True, 2024).

4 Kimberly Firth et al., "Healing, a Concept Analysis," *Global Advances in Health and Medicine* 4, no. 6 (2015): 49, https://www.doi.org/10.7453/gahmj.2015.056.

5 Linda Crockett is the founder and consultant for Safe Communities in Lancaster, PA, https://www.safecommunitiespa.org.

6 Lyn Barrett, *Crazy: Reclaiming Life from the Shadow of Traumatic Memory* (Koehler Books, 2022).

7 Barrett, *Crazy*, 104.

8 Joseph Campbell and Bill Moyers, *The Power of Myth* (Anchor Books, 1991).

9 T. S. Eliot, "Little Gidding," *Four Quartets* (Harcourt, Brace, and Co., 1943).

10 Suritaplus, *Quilted: Piecing Together My Dissociated Selves* (pub. by author, 2023).

11 Anastasia Pollock, "Why I Don't Use the Word 'Forgiveness' in Trauma Therapy," *Good Therapy* (2016): https://www.goodtherapy.org/blog/why-i-dont-use-the-word-forgiveness-in-trauma-therapy-0120164.

12 Maria Mayo, *The Limits of Forgiveness: Case Studies in the Distortion of a Biblical Ideal* (Wipf and Stock, 2015).

13 Susannah Griffith, *Forgiveness After Trauma: A Path to Find Healing and Empowerment* (Brazos Press, 2024).

14 Suzanne R. Friedman and Robert Enright, "Forgiveness As an Intervention Goal with Incest Survivors," *Journal of Consulting and Clinical Psychology* 64, no. 5 (1996): https://psycnet.apa.org/buy/1996-00478-019.

15 Fred Luskin, *Forgive for Good: A Proven Prescription for Health and Happiness* (Harper One, 2002), 43.

16 Jeanne M. Slattery, "A Time and Place for Forgiveness," *The Pennsylvania Psychologist* 8, (2019): 79.

17 Luskin, *Forgive for Good*, viii.

18 Janis Abrahms Spring, *How Can I Forgive You? The Courage to Forgive, the Freedom Not To* (Harper, 2004).

19 Robert D. Enright, *Forgiveness Is a Choice: A Step-by-Step Process for Resolving Anger and Restoring Hope* (American Psychological Association, 2001), 166.

20 Diane Pomerantz, "Is Forgiveness Necessary for Healing? Is It Really a Prerequisite to Healing from Abuse?" *Psychology Today* (2021): https://www.psychologytoday.com/us/blog/lost-in-the-reflecting-pool/202101/is-forgiveness-necessary-healing.

21 Spring, *How Can I Forgive You*? 35.

22 David Bedrick, JD, "6 Reasons Not to Forgive, Not Yet," *Psychology Today* (2014): https://www.psychologytoday.com/us/blog/is-psychology-making-us-sick/201409/6-reasons-not-forgive-not-yet.

23 Enright, *Forgiveness Is a Choice*, 18.

24 Slattery, "A Time and Place for Forgiveness."

25 Barrett, *Crazy*, 117.

26 "Ritual abuse is 'a calculated, systematic process whereby victims may be brainwashed and programmed, using many different techniques, to disown and distort our own sense of self and reality.' In such abuse, 'triggers' and programming may have been placed around primary biological and survival functions, including eating, sleeping, breathing, sexuality, elimination, emotions, the five senses, and human bonding. Victims may have been forced and manipulated into breaking primary bonds to survive emotionally and physically. This may have involved forced participation in the torture,

murder, dismemberment, and cannibalism of animals and humans that victims may have known and even loved." US Department of Justice (1994). *Understanding Ritual Abuse: A Guide for Self-Empowerment for Ritual Abuse Survivors.*

27 Pete Walker, *The Tao of Fully Feeling: Harvesting Forgiveness Out of Blame* (Azure Coyote Publishing, 1995), 11.

28 Walker, *The Tao of Fully Feeling*, 206.

29 Janina Fisher, *Transforming the Living Legacy of Trauma: A Workbook for Survivors and Therapists* (PESI Publishing,1921), 105.

30 Jamie Marich, *You Lied to Me About God: A Memoir* (North Atlantic Books, 2024).

31 Find the referenced directories at the following links: https://directory.multipliedbyone.org/, https://www.psychologytoday.com/ca/therapists/dissociative-disorders, https://isstd.connectedcommunity.org/network/network-find-a-professional

32 Judith L. Herman, *Trauma and Recovery: The Aftermath of Violence—From Domestic Abuse to Political Terror* (Basic Books, 1992).

33 Bonnie R. Armstrong, *An Apparently Normal Person* (Emerald Lake Books, 2024).

34 Bessel van der Kolk, *The Body Keeps the Score: Brain, Mind, and Body in the Healing of Trauma* (Viking, 2014), 176.

35 Fisher, *Transforming the Living Legacy of Trauma*, 13.

36 Fisher, *Transforming the Living Legacy of Trauma*, 23.

37 Fisher, *Transforming the Living Legacy of Trauma*, 2.

38 Olga R. Trujillo, *The Sum of My Parts: A Survivor's Story of Dissociative Identity Disorder* (New Harbinger Publications, 2011).

39 Shelley Kolton, *Brain Storm: A Life in Pieces* (FLR Press, 2021).

40 Brené Brown, "Shame vs. Guilt," January 15, 2013, https://brenebrown.com/articles/2013/01/15/shame-v-guilt/.

41 Fisher, *Transforming the Living Legacy of Trauma*, 25–26.

42 Elizabeth Kübler-Ross, *On Death and Dying* (The Macmillan Company, 1969).

43 Cathy Collyer, *Staying in the Room: Managing Medical and Dental Care When You Have DID*, (pub. by author, 2021).

44 Barrett, *Crazy*, 107.

45 Fisher, *Transforming the Living Legacy of Trauma*, 1.

46 Fisher, *Transforming the Living Legacy of Trauma*, 1.

47 Carolyn Spring, *Recovery Is My Best Revenge* (Carolyn Spring Publishing, 2014).

48 Find the referenced resources at www.dissociativewriters.com and www.aninfinitemind.com

49 Barrett, *Crazy*, 12.

50 Ronald Rolheiser, *The Holy Longing: The Search for a Christian Spirituality* (Doubleday, 1999).

51 "Ground of being" is a phrase coined by theologian Paul Tillich (1886–1965), usually referring to what most of us would call God ("In him we live and move and have our being." Acts 17:28a).

52 Barrett, *Crazy*, 187.

53 Barrett, *Crazy*, 189.

54 Lyn Barrett, "Integration vs. Functional Multiplicity," https://www.lynbarrett.com/blog/integration-vs-functional-multiplicity, and "Integrated or Functionally Multiple?" https://www.lynbarrett.com/blog/integrated-or-functionally-multiple.

55 Helen Keller, *Let Us Have Faith* (Doubleday and Company, 1940), 51.

56 Griffith, *Forgiveness After Trauma*, 110.

57 Mayo, *The Limits of Forgiveness*, 7.

58 Mayo, *The Limits of Forgiveness*, 11.

59 Mayo, *The Limits of Forgiveness*, 1.

60 Private communication with Friar Peter Chepaitis, OFM, Bethany Ministries, Middleburgh, NY, January 28, 2025.

www.ingramcontent.com/pod-product-compliance
Lightning Source LLC
LaVergne TN
LVHW060036210926
848481LV00013B/3882